JUSTIFIABLE HOMICIDE?

JUSTIFIABLE HOMICIDE?

The Radical Scheme To Destroy A Race

A. C. BOLCHOZ, PE, MS

JUSTIFIABLE HOMICIDE?

Copyright © 2017 by A. C. Bolchoz, PE, MS

Paperback ISBN: 978-1-944212-38-4
eBook ISBN: 978-1-944212-39-1

Printed in the United States of America
16 17 18 19 20 21 LSI 9 8 7 6 5 4 3 2 1

CONTENTS

DEDICATION

This book is dedicated to every child that has suffered because good men failed to act.

ACKNOWLEDGMENTS

I would like to acknowledge the support of my mother, Christie, Paul, Javier, Zildo, Jose Manual, Francisco and Pamela, without whom this book would have not been possible.

INTRODUCTION

A justifiable homicide is "that which is committed with the intention to kill or to do a grievous bodily injury, under circumstances which the law holds sufficient to exculpate the person who commits it."[1]

Currently, from an international legal standpoint there are very few instances of acceptable forms of justifiable homicide, nonetheless they do exist. Possibly the most obvious example would be the right of an official charged with maintaining peace to defend himself and the public from bodily harm. Another example is the privilege of an individual to defend his person and property, although this concept varies in accordance with the jurisdictional laws of the region in question. There is also a case of justifiable homicide that does not depend on the response to a belligerent action at a particular moment. The death penalty being exercised by a sovereign state is one particular example. Here, the justification of the killing of a person is based on the perceived threat the person presents not to a particular person but to society in general.

It is obvious that a justifiable homicide should only be promoted as a last resort against a person that is seen as sufficient threat to other person(s). Also, by logical inference the justification of killing another person implies an implicit guilt on the part of the person being killed. On the other hand, the person who defends his life is considered innocent and therefore is not legally liable for the killing of a person in self-defense. Thus, the justification of a homicide depends on the right to protect an innocent life which is derived directly from the concept of an innate "right to life" that each person has.

This right to defend one's life, or *self-preservation*, is a basic feature of the majority of human moral thought. Evidence of this concept of self-preservation can be found in many international laws. One such example is article four of the "Universal Declaration of Human Rights" by the United Nations which states[2]:

Everyone has the right to life, liberty and security of person.

It is clearly evident then that there is a universal moral standard that each human being has an innate *right to life* which by logical projection permits a legitimate, mortal, and personal defense in response to grave and deadly situations without fear of legal repercussion.

In summary, justified homicide would only seem to be applicable for certain cases involving a person who has or would harm another person. However, what if this is not actually the case? What if a form of justifiable homicide of innocent people is now being promoted in parts of the world? The surprising reality is that the killing of innocent persons is indeed being promoted using United States and European Union tax dollars. This book will discuss the clear reasoning behind such sponsorship and will reveal a large void in the very foundation of the Western legal system that has in turn mandated such propaganda. Selected social indicators from United Nations data will be presented as evidence that will bring to light information that no Western country would knowingly promote, thus supporting the notion that there is a real impetus for the West to promote the justifiable homicide of innocent persons beyond its borders.

CHAPTER ONE

RIGHTS OF THE INDIVIDUAL; FOUNDATION OF WESTERN DEMOCRACY AND IMPETUS FOR CHANGE

Of all the forms of government in recorded history the general perception is the democratic forms are considered the most superior. The reasoning is that democracies give voice to its citizens and as such are the least susceptible to gross abuses and corruption such as high taxes, repressive or non-representative laws and violence, all of which have been a regular feature of political systems throughout human history.

The foundation of the democratic system is based on the principal that the individual has certain innate rights. These rights in turn are manifested in privileges and laws. Some examples are the right of the citizen to participate in the everyday governance of the jurisdictional authority where he resides, the freedom of speech, the ownership of property and perhaps most significant, the right to life. This is clearly different from many other forms of government where little importance is given to the rights of the populace to participate in the decision-making process nor much less the recognition of basic human rights. In fact, historians suggest democracy arose in response to tyrannical systems of government with few individual rights.

One such example of an early democracy was the city-state of Athens in Ancient Greece which historians believe arose in response to the harsh laws created under the Draconian constitution. It is understood the notion of a *citizen* started with the Athenian model. The term *polis*, as in *Acropolis/Metropolis*, came to mean the jurisdictional unit as well as the body of citizens that comprise the aforementioned unit. Not surprisingly philosophy emerged as a discipline during this same period. The *father* of philosophy, Thales of Miletus, attempted to understand natural phenomenon without the need to defer to mythology. It is quite possible this was in reaction to the perception that mythology was a form of propaganda used to control the populace. It would appear that this approach to questioning the status quo eventually manifested itself in questions regarding morality. For example, Socrates struggled with the issue of personal and societal morality. In Plato's "The Republic" Socrates discusses the essence of a *just man* with Polemarcus:[1]

> *Then won't we say the same about human beings, too, that when they are harmed they become worse in human virtue?*
>
> *Indeed.*
>
> *But isn't justice human virtue?*
>
> *Yes, certainly.*
>
> *Then people who are harmed must become more unjust?*

So it seems . . .

. . . Then, Polemarchus, it isn't the function of a just person to harm a friend or anyone else, rather it is the function of his opposite, an unjust person?

In my view that's completely true, Socrates.

If anyone tells us, then, that it is just to give to each what he's owed and understands by this that a just man should harm his enemies and benefit his friends, he isn't wise to say it, since what he says isn't true, for it has become clear to us that it is never just to harm anyone?

Here Socrates makes it clear that the just man would never do wrong to another person regardless of the person's virtue or lack of. In other words, the just man's actions are not dependent on his treatment by others. Socrates thus proposed a moral standard for individuals where doing wrong can never be justified, even in response to an unjust action. Interestingly, this concept would appear to be somewhat unique in the region based on historical evidence. For example, *The Code of Hammurabi*, which was developed more than a thousand years prior in nearby Babylonia, sustains a different perspective regarding addressing wrongs committed against innocent persons. Here is an excerpt from Laws 196 and 197[2]:

If a man put out the eye of another man, his eye shall be put out . . .

If he break another man's bone, his bone shall be broken.

Similarly, from the Judaic tradition during the time of Moses we see something very similar (Ex. 21:23–25, NABRE):

But if injury ensues, you shall give life for life, eye for eye, tooth for tooth, hand for hand, foot for foot, burn for burn, wound for wound, stripe for stripe.

It is apparent Socrates concept of a just man responding to bad deeds with good is a departure from the traditional norm.

Socrates idea of a just man in a society is where each person has a right to live their life in peace unharmed by others. This is of course a basic precept of the concept of the rights of the individual as it has consistently been interpreted by modern democratic societies.

To continue, while the city-state of Athens of Ancient Greece is considered the first democracy by scholars the Roman Republic also was distinguished by having a representative form of government as well. Here we see the emergence of the *plebs*, or free Roman citizens, in the political arena at the expense of the *patricians*, the aristocracy derived from important and wealthy families. One important consequence of this political conflict was a set of civil laws; the "Twelve Tables". According to historical accounts this was a concession to free citizens increasingly at odds with the ruling patricians.[3] Eventually this group of free Roman citizens was also granted the right to pass "plebiscites" (balloted bills) as well. Ultimately the ever-increasing struggle of power between the plebs and the patricians caused the emergence of a separate noble class whereby nobility was determined by tenure and family connections. It is apparent that the representative form of government grew in importance in direct proportion to the increasing rights demanded by ordinary citizens who, in turn, demanded more and more recognition of their rights. While it is true the Roman Republic experimented with dictatorships the tradition of a representative form of government became an established component of the Roman political landscape. In fact, the Roman Republic eventually became the Roman Empire which maintained certain vestiges of the representative system, specifically the Senate. The Roman Empire of course has had a great deal of effect on Western political thought due in no small part to the development of the rights of the individual as an essential feature.

Of equal importance to the development of the Western concept of individual rights was Christianity. This was due in part to its emphasis on the rights of the individual to live his life in peace. In fact, in "Sermon on the Mount" Jesus Christ proclaims (Matt. 6, NABRE):

> *Blessed are the peacemakers, for they will be called children of God . . .*
>
> *. . . Therefore, if you bring your gift to the altar, and there recall that your brother has anything against you, leave your gift there at the altar, go first and be reconciled with your brother, and then come and offer your gift. Settle with your opponent quickly while on the way to court with him . . .*
>
> *. . . But I say to you, love your enemies, and pray for those who persecute you . . .*

Here we see that Christianity would promote a standard of behavior that proposes that individuals should respond to acts of wrongdoing with acts of forgiveness and goodwill. This stance is a clear departure from the "eye for an eye" commandment that was an integral part of the Judaic ethical code, but instead is very similar to Socrates' philosophy. In effect this new moral code elevated even further the concept of the rights of the individual by setting a standard that would seem to limit the pursuit of justice to a very narrow parameter. This relation between this novel norm and personal rights may not be apparent at first glance but given the following verse from the same book (Matt. 22, NABRE), we see the underlying purpose of this directive:

> *"Teacher, which commandment in the law is the greatest?"*
> *He said to him, "You shall love the Lord, your God, with all your heart, with all your soul, and with all your mind. This is the greatest and the first commandment. The second is like it: You shall love your neighbor as yourself. The whole law and the prophets depend on these two commandments.*

Here we see that the motive for tolerating offenses committed by others is based on concept of brotherly love that prioritizes the right of the individual to not be harmed for any reason, even at the expense of justice.

As previously mentioned, Socrates promoted this same philosophy in his writings. Socrates recognized the positive effects of such principles where wrongs are resolved with little fanfare and where people are willing to suffer injustices for the greater societal benefit of fraternity and peace; in other words, the right of the individual to not be harmed for his transgressions subordinates justice for the sake of the community. While it is true that Socrates' and the Christian models of subordinating justice to the right of the individual to not be harmed were not exactly embraced nonetheless it is important to recognize this proposed elevation of individual rights was significant for their respective time periods.

To continue, initially the Roman Empire saw Christianity as a threat and mercilessly killed Christians for more than a century. Eventually the Roman Emperor Constantine granted certain rights to Christianity thus ending its state sponsored persecution. After the partition of the Roman Empire, the Western branch gradually crumbled in the fifth century. The remaining Eastern Roman Empire in Constantinople was in existence for more than millennia.

Up until the fall of the Western Roman Empire we see Greek and Roman legal and political traditions growing out of a need to accommodate an increasingly important societal class, the free citizen. Different representative political methods have been utilized but the common thread has been the constant struggle for power of the common man with the aristocracy and/or dictators. After this period, we see a continuation of Roman law being developed but not necessarily through one particular government. Rather this maturity occurs through various governments throughout Western and Eastern Europe in conjunction with the now popular Christian morality. In fact, with the gradual disintegration of the Western Roman Empire the Catholic Church was left to fill the void with its doctrine combined with Roman Law.[4] There was also similar mutual interactions between the early Catholic Church doctrine and the Eastern Roman Empire after the promulgation of the Code of Justinian in the 6th century. In fact, one historian states: [5]

For it should never be forgotten that the Canon law was the medium through which the Christian Church aided the preservation of Roman Civil law to modern times. "The

*laws of Justinian have been woven into the fabric of the
Canon law and in that form . . . obtained the sanction of
the church."*

In Western Europe, the emergence of the Holy Roman
Empire in the ninth century continued the process of
developing Western political thought until its dissolution in
the nineteenth century. Even after the Catholic Church started
to lose political influence in other parts of Europe during the
Middle Ages the Canon Law still made its effect felt as secular
civil courts used it as a basis for their legal system.[6]

At the end of the Middle Ages, with the secularization of
some governments (the rejection of the once predominant
authority of the Roman Catholic Church) there arose a secular
movement which focused on the rights of the individual. This
would appear to be a continuation of the now fully intertwined
Christian morality with Western thought but with no official
connection to the Roman Catholic Church. This period is
considered the beginning of the modern Western political
thought as it is understood today.

One of the most renowned philosophers of the
Enlightenment was John Locke, an Englishman. He was
considered the father of classical liberalism and also an
advocate of *individualism*, where the rights of the individual are
paramount. This is clearly evident in the following statements:[7]

> *. . . no one ought to harm another in his life, health, liberty,
> or possessions . . .*

> *. . . or have a mind to unite, for the mutual preservation
> of their lives, liberties and estates . . .*

While the Age of Enlightenment flourished in Europe, the Glorious Revolution of England in 1688 established a parliamentary democracy that remains to this day. Some historians claim Lockean liberalism was an influencing factor in this important historic event. Whether this is true or not it is interesting that the following year the Bill of Rights of 1689 was promulgated in England which further established the importance of the rights of the individual. Historians also believe Locke's views on the civil rights was a basis for the laws of the first modern secular democracy: The United States of America.

Individual rights were of such importance to the Founding Fathers that they considered any encroachment on these rights as cause for the dissolution of the government. This reality is apparent in the following excerpt from the American Declaration of Independence:[8]

We hold these truths to be self-evident, that all men are created equal, that they are endowed by their Creator with certain unalienable Rights, that among these are Life, Liberty and the pursuit of Happiness.

-- That to secure these rights, Governments are instituted among Men, deriving their just powers from the consent of the governed, -- That whenever any Form of Government becomes destructive of these ends, it is the Right of the People to alter or to abolish it . . .

Due to this unique feature of subordinating the rights of the government to the rights of the individual a new dynamic process was created whereby new laws are constantly being created and/or modified at the will of the constituents in order to satisfy the prime directive of eliminating infringements of individual rights.

A clear example of this dynamic is the issue of slavery in the US. The institution of slavery was still common in the late 1700s when American colonialists were planning their independence from Great Britain, after all it was something the British had brought to the colonies. It would seem logical that slavery would have to be abolished as well, since there were few other individual rights abuses worse than slavery. In fact, Thomas Jefferson thought so and apparently planned to have slavery abolished for the proposed United States of America. In the rough draft of the Declaration of Independence Jefferson called slavery:[9]

> . . . a cruel war against human nature.

This seemed perfectly logical to Jefferson given that he had also written:[10]

> We hold these truths to be self-evident, that all men are created equal, that they are endowed by their Creator with certain unalienable Rights, that among these are Life, Liberty and the pursuit of Happiness.

Nonetheless, the slaveholder delegates to the Continental Congress objected to the prohibition of slavery for obvious reasons and the statement was removed.[11] Consequently, this created a conflict which was then left to subsequent politicians and lawmakers to address.

One of the first cases to address the question of slavery was *Brom and Bett v. Ashley* in the state of Massachusetts in 1781.[12] This case was significant in that the supposition was that slavery was deemed to be in conflict with the recent adoption of the state constitution in which "all men are born free and equal."[13] The Supreme Court of Massachusetts, in fact, did rule that slavery was illegal and awarded the former slaves their freedom while also compensating them for damages. The basis of this decision of course was the logical recognition of the innate and natural rights of slaves as individuals to be free using the state constitution as reference. The defendant in this case, the slaveholder, was deemed to not have any rights at all to enslave a fellow human being. In effect the slaveowners' right to enslave another person was subordinated by the slave's right to freedom and consequently rendered null and void.

Subsequently with the passage of the Act Prohibiting Importation of Slaves in 1807, it would appear that the beginning of the end slavery in the US was near given that at least one state abolished slavery and the Federal government stopped the legal importation of slaves but unfortunately this was not the case of course.[14] The North Carolina case *State v. Mann* in 1829 had a completely different outcome than the earlier case in Massachusetts.[15] Here the State tried to prosecute a slave owner who had severely harmed one of his slaves. Nonetheless, the court ruled the slave had no rights as an individual. In spite of this ruling the presiding judge in the matter, Thomas Ruffin, was obviously conflicted as he actually admitted that he sympathized with the slave.[16] This decision demonstrates a situation where a judge of a high court rejected his natural instinct that a human being's right to be free should be given precedence over all other interests.

One has to question the logic of the verdict given its disagreement with the principles of the creation of the United States of America as demonstrated in the Declaration of Independence. Perhaps Ruffin was not aware of the Massachusetts decision or maybe because of the undoubtedly overwhelming public opinion in favor of slavery in North Carolina at that time he felt compelled to lean to the majority opinion. What is certain is this case reveals a reality confronting issues regarding the prioritization of rights in that they could be subject to pressure from public opinion, party affiliation, uninformed notions or personal prejudices.

There were many other cases argued as well, mostly in state courts with the majority of the decisions being against slavery. In spite of this fact, the 1857 landmark US Supreme Court case *Dred Scott v. Sanford* ruled blacks could never be US Citizens and thus was considered a major setback for abolitionists.[17] However, it also polarized public opinion on the matter and helped Abraham Lincoln secure a presidential bid as an anti-slavery candidate. Shortly afterwards in 1860 Lincoln was elected president which provoked various southern states to secede from the Union. This in turn caused the Civil War. Lincoln subsequently abolished slavery via the Emancipation Proclamation, thus elevating the rights of the enslaved person to the equal of all other Americans while the rights of the slaveholder were summarily dismissed.

Lincoln's actions to resolve the inherent conflict between allowing slavery in a system built on individual rights was a bold maneuver and, in fact, was predictable recognizing the dynamic process of the prioritization of rights. Nevertheless, the equal recognition of black rights would not be addressed in any capacity for more than a century due to various setbacks. Specifically, the promulgation of Jim Crow laws and the Ku Klux Klan by the Democrat Party limited blacks' participation in politics by law and terror as well as segregation. However, as would be expected in a Western system founded on individual rights at some point this issue would have to be confronted. One of the more important cases in the increased recognition of blacks' rights was the federal court case *Brown v. Board of Education*. The issue at hand was the constitutionality of segregated public schools. In this particular case the Supreme Court ruled segregated public schools were indeed not in line with the spirit of the constitution.[18] This is generally considered the beginning of the civil rights movement in the United States, which eventually culminated with the Civil Rights Acts of 1964 and 1968. These acts would officially integrate blacks into American society by law and give them all of the privileges afforded to white citizens, thus fulfilling the inevitable ideological mandate of prioritizing the rights of blacks over all other belligerent challengers. It is noteworthy to point out that the nature of this particular individual right, the recognition that blacks are human, is that it cannot be rescinded given the ideological barrier to any such proposition. In other words, once a *truth* is revealed about an individual right's innate precedence in the Western system it cannot be rejected, only superseded by other rights. Furthermore, the right of a person to be recognized as human is among the most basic inherent rights. Therefore, by this measure the right of blacks to be considered human would easily defeat all challengers and would have to be considered permanent.

Up to this point we have reviewed the ideological origin of the Western concept of individual rights as well as its evolution over the course of history. Using the United States as a prime example of the political manifestation of this concept, we have witnessed the volatile and ever changing prioritization of individual rights over the course of its relatively recent history.

By recognizing the underlying dynamics of the prioritization process and its corresponding ideological impetus we can then see that the United States' progression in regard to individual rights is in fact predictable. It can even be considered an expected outcome. Furthermore, we see that once a basic individual right is recognized it would remain so indefinitely.

In the next chapter we will discuss an issue of individual rights that is still in a process of *prioritization* but one that is being manipulated by political interests in much the same way the issue of slavery was in the United States. Similarly, if the normal process of recognizing the innate rights of this particular group of people is squelched, the United States will once again be led to the brink. At a minimum, the short term consequences would be the United States relinquishing its cherished role as a moral authority in the world.

CHAPTER TWO

HUMAN LIFE LEGISLATION: THE ACHILLES HEEL OF THE WEST

In the previous chapter, we see that the foundation of modern democracies is the concept of individuals' rights which in turn mandates the prioritization of certain individual rights while others are subordinated or even invalidated. A good example is the historical case of the right to have a slave versus the right of the slave to be free. In this particular example we saw there was a clear progression of awareness of the rights of the black man, which in turn mandated the invalidation of the erroneous notion that a black person was not human. This advancement of thought was influenced not only by Abolitionists, who generally used the Bible as an authoritative source, but also by significant philosophers from the Enlightenment period, such as Montesquieu. Let's now look at the similarities of the progression of the abortion debate keeping in mind what we observed in the slavery debate.

Abortion is mentioned in texts from ancient Greece, Roman and Israel. The Jewish bible considered the killing of a child in the womb to be punishable by death. The Greek Hippocratic Oath forbade abortion, which is significant because this oath was relevant in Rome, even before its conversion to Christianity, and remained intact for more than two thousand years.

The Catholic Church has always had a consistent stance against abortion since its very inception. This is understandable given the Judaic tradition regarding the status of the unborn child, as demonstrated in the following verses:

> *Before I formed you in the womb I knew you, before you were born I dedicated you, a prophet to the nations I appointed you* (Jer. 1:5, NAB).

The verse clearly establishes that a child is recognized from the very beginning of his formation in the womb. Below is a common verse used to condemn as well as justify abortion in English and the original Latin Vulgate:[1]

> *When men have a fight and hurt a pregnant woman, so that she suffers a miscarriage, but no further injury, the guilty one shall be fined as much as the woman's husband demands of him, and he shall pay in the presence of the judges. But if injury ensues, you shall give life for life, eye for eye, tooth for tooth, hand for hand, foot for foot* (Ex. 21:22–25, VUL).

> *Sin autem uno die vel duobus supervixerit, non subjacebit poenae, quia pecunia illius est. Si rixati fuerint viri, et percusserit quis mulierem praegnantem, et abortivum quidem fecerit, sed ipsa vixerit: subjacebit damno quantum maritus mulieris expetierit, et arbitri judicaverint. Sin autem mors ejus fuerit subsecuta, reddet animam pro anima, oculum pro oculo, dentem pro dente, manum pro*

manu, pedem pro pede, adustionem pro adustione, vulnus pro vulnere, livorem pro livore.

In the English and original Latin Vulgate at first glance it might appear there is a possible ambiguity in the original due to the term "miscarriage" (abortivum), which could mean death or premature birth. However, when taken in context with the verse from Jeremiah it becomes clear that a person is recognized by God even before they are conceived and as such the term "miscarriage" in this particular verse must refer to a premature birth, and thus requires only a fine as recompense, while the death of the child would require taking the life of the assailant. The Bible consistently uses multiple verses as a type of literary practice in order to give a multi-faceted perspective to concepts or positions.

The New Testament also has other relevant examples that demonstrate that life was recognized at conception such as the following verse:

And the angel said to her in reply, "The holy Spirit will come upon you, and the power of the Most High will overshadow you. Therefore, the child to be born will be called holy, the Son of God. And behold, Elizabeth, your relative, has also conceived a son in her old age, and this is the sixth month for her who was called barren; for nothing will be impossible for God." Mary said, "Behold, I am the handmaid of the Lord. May it be done to me according to your word." Then the angel departed from her. During those days Mary set out and traveled to the hill country in haste to a town of Judah, where she entered the house of Zechariah and greeted Elizabeth. When Elizabeth heard Mary's greeting, the infant leaped in her womb, and

Elizabeth, filled with the holy Spirit, cried out in a loud voice and said, "Most blessed are you among women, and blessed is the fruit of your womb (Luke 1:35–42, NAB).

There were also many discussions within the Catholic Church from the very beginning of its existence that reveal the Catholic Church's stance that life is recognized at conception and in fact must be protected.[2]

"You shall love your neighbor more than your own life. You shall not slay the child by abortion" Barnabas (c. 70–138), Epistle, Volume II, page 19.

"You shall not kill an unborn child or murder a newborn infant." The Didache ("The Lord's Instruction to the Gentiles through the Twelve Apostles"). II, 2, translated by J.A. Kleist, S.J., Ancient Christian Writers, Volume 6. Westminster, 1948, page 16.

"Those women who use drugs to bring about an abortion commit murder and will have to give an account to God for their abortion." Athenagoras of Athens, letter to Marcus Aurelius in 177, Legatio pro Christianis ("Supplication for the Christians"), page 35.

"Some virgins [unmarried women], when they learn they are with child through sin, practice abortion by the use of drugs. Frequently they die themselves and are brought before the ruler of the lower world guilty of three crimes; suicide, adultery against Christ, and murder of an unborn child." St. Jerome, Bible Scholar and translator (c. 340–420), Letter to Eustochium, 22.13.

"Concerning women who commit fornication, and destroy that which they have conceived, or who are employed in making drugs for abortion, a former decree excluded them until the hour of death, and to this some have assented. Nevertheless, being desirous to use somewhat greater lenity, we have ordained that they fulfill ten years [of penance], according to the prescribed degrees." Council of Ancyracanon 21, (AD 314).

Nonetheless, while the Catholic Church consistently considered all abortions equivalent to murder for more than a thousand years subsequently some influential persons in the Church revisited the concept of "delayed animation" in the High Middle Ages. It is believed St. Thomas Aquinas promotion of Aristotle's concept of the body of a person being conceived without a soul (which would be infused at some later date, i.e. "ensoulment") had some influence on this decision. This "delayed animation" concept was introduced to the "Decretum Gratiani" in the twelfth century, which was later incorporated into the "Corpus Juris Canonici," a canonical reference.[3] From the point of view of this particular doctrinal reference abortion before a child's body was animated was not considered homicide, which would create a conflict between the centuries old Catholic teaching established directly from sacred Scripture. The conflict between those who viewed all abortions as homicide, *traditionalists*, and those who only viewed abortions after ensoulment as homicide, *animationists*, would play out over the subsequent centuries.

Many questions have been raised about the possible impact of the aforementioned doctrinal document, with some authors suggesting that the Church resolutely adopted the animation doctrine while discarding the traditionalist stance completely. Before delving into the historical evidence to address this claim it makes sense to point out a few obvious points. First, while the "Decretum Gratiani" declared that abortions before animation were not considered homicide this did nothing to change the status that all abortions after animation were still considered homicide. Furthermore, even though abortions before animation were not considered the equivalent of homicide this does not mean that abortion was considered a lesser sin, on the contrary, it was still considered the destruction of a person, albeit without a soul and as such the forgiveness of such a serious sin was not granted to local priests.[4]

Let's now look into the evidence that draws into question the affirmation that the ensoulment theory effectively displaced the well-established traditionalist stance that all abortions were the equivalent of homicide.

The existence of conflicting theories is nothing new in the Catholic Church but rather has been a common feature throughout much of its history. After all, when the Church was formed some two thousand years ago there was no codified doctrine and as such it would have to be developed. The creation of doctrine is a dynamic process whereby new theories are submitted and pass a process of review by Church theologians and leaders, something that can take centuries. Obviously, significant periods of time can pass where conflicting doctrines coexist. This would obviously create a predicament given that some church leaders would choose to defer to the original doctrine while other leaders would defer to the newer, challenger theory. Eventually one of the conflicting doctrinal stances would have to be discarded (which is precisely what happened to the challenger ensoulment theory).

Furthermore, while it is true the ensoulment theory survived various centuries when one considers a few factors it becomes clear why this particular case would have lingered. Firstly, one must take into account the state of the propagation of information at this time given that the printing press would not be invented for another three hundred years. It is also important to note the extent of the influence of the Roman Catholic Church, which occupied a considerable amount of area of Western Europe from the Baltic to the Mediterranean Seas. It is apparent the inherently slow rate of the duplication of Church documents would have directly affected this particular doctrine's dissemination, and subsequently its exposure to criticism within the Church. Secondly, the limited knowledge of the biologic process of conception during this time period as well as the fact that St. Augustine as well as St. Thomas more supported the animation theory would have allowed the animation theory to survive until the Church could affect a vigorous review. Thirdly, given the historically very low incidence of abortion (as we shall see in a later chapter) the topic of abortion would not have been approached in public forums if not absolutely necessary, therefore delaying the necessity of addressing the conflicting animation theory when there were much more pressing issues to resolve at hand.

As previously mentioned, the disagreement between the animationists and traditionalists was only the question of the recognition of abortion as homicide before the point of animation of the fetus as after this point both parties agreed that abortion was murder. Also, the classification of homicide by animationists would have been at the forty-day point of gestation for all cases due to the obvious reality that there was no way to determine the sex of the fetus due to the limited understanding of the pregnancy process. This observation is important in order to understand when one recognizes the probable source of early-term abortions and the inherent conflict that doomed the animation theory to failure even before it was adopted.

Women accused of witchcraft have long been associated with abortion. The *Malleus Maleficarum* (Hammer of the Witches) is a valuable source created by the Catholic Church at the request of Pope Innocent VIII by means of the Papal Bull "Summis desiderantes affectibus" in 1484. The "Malleus Maleficarum" was created to be a guide for Inquisitors in order to recognize and prosecute witches for various offenses, including abortion:[5]

> *Witches are not content with such practices in respect of the genital member, causing some prestidigitatory illusion of its disappearance (although this disappearance is not an actual fact); but they even frequently take away the generative power itself, so that a woman cannot conceive, and a man cannot perform the act even when he still retains his member. And without any illusion, they also cause abortion after conception, often accompanied with many other ills.*

Women accused of witchcraft were considered a primary source of potions that were effective in causing abortions during the early stages of pregnancy, as inferred in the above excerpt. This is significant because we know that hiding a pregnancy at the time was construed as criminal intent to procure an abortion. This is evident from King Henry II's edict of the same time period (1556):[6]

... many women with child by dishonesty or other means, have been persuaded by persons of ill will and malice to disguise, conceal and hide their pregnancies leaving nothing to discover and declare ...

Therefore, witches would have been sought out by women desiring abortions shortly after their first absent menstrual period in order to not run the risk of attempting an abortion after visibly showing signs of being pregnant. Taking into account this logical observation with the fact that the "Malleus Maleficarum" recognized abortions after conception with no mention of the status of animation and it is clear women accused of witchcraft would have been charged with abortion before animation. Furthermore, severe punishments were called for to include torture and burning at the stake, which was a standard practice in Catholic kingdoms that stretched back to Roman times.[7] Thus we can be sure that witches were most certainly being executed at this time for procuring abortions, in spite of the fact that the animation theory was considered by some in the Catholic Church to be doctrine.

It appears clear that the "Malleus Maleficarum" was a purposeful act by the traditionalist element in the Catholic Church to affirm the Church's right to prosecute early term abortions provoked by witches. After all this historical evidence shows this had been done for centuries given that women accused of witchcraft were a prime source of abortifacients.

The assertion that abortions were prosecuted by Catholic Kingdoms during this period is further confirmed by the (aforementioned) declaration by King Henry II of France in 1556 that declared all abortions were considered homicide and subject to the death penalty.[8]

Shortly after King Henry's declaration Pope Sixtus V issued the Papa Bull "Effraenatam" in 1588 which once again officially equated all abortions with murder.[9] Nonetheless, shortly thereafter in 1591 Pope Gregory XIV annulled Pope Sixtus V's bull due to the severity of the punishment effected by Catholic governments who used Church doctrine as civil law, thus allowing the ensoulment theory to stand.[10]

In spite of the apparent setback the traditionalists were not to be dissuaded. The "Malleus Maleficarum" would continue to be used for more than a century by Catholic Clergy and kingdoms alike, in apparent direct contradiction to Pope Gregory XIV's decision. Also, France did not change its civil code to accommodate this supposed reversion to the animation theory but instead continued prosecuting all abortions as capital offenses. In fact, King Louis XIV publically reaffirmed King Henri II's edict in 1708 which no doubt endured until the French Revolution.[11] The same abortion-as-murder tradition was reaffirmed in France after the Revolution with the adoption of the French Penal code of 1810.[12]

Spain too created laws like France at the turn of the nineteenth century that considered all abortions as homicide as seen in its penal code. [13]

Eventually Pope Pius IX once and for all did away with the conflicting teachings of ensoulment in 1869, although it would be a matter of years before any references to pre-animated states of fetus would be removed from the removed from the Corpus Juris Canonici.[14]

It is quite evident that while the animation doctrine was considered valid the traditionalist element in the Church was never displaced, nor poorly represented for that matter, but in fact promulgated guidelines and laws that clearly ignored the animation doctrine. Thus, is it is clear that there was a battle of wills between traditionalists and animationists among Church hierarchy and governments during the most active years of the animation discussion.

Taking this into account, when we see that Pope Sixtus V's papal bull was struck down not due to opposition of the doctrinal stance that animated children are created at conception but rather because of an excessiveness of punishments we should suspect that the original reason the ensoulment theory was revisited and subsequently accepted as doctrine was to limit Catholic kingdoms from being overly aggressive in their targeting of women accused of witchery. After all the animation theory arose at the time of the Medieval Inquisitions.

The evidence points to the Catholic Church allowing the animation theory to temporarily survive due to various factors. Nonetheless, it is clear that the ensoulment theory never displaced the much more traditional stance that all abortions were homicide. The real impact of the animation theory on Catholic society was even less significant given the innate low incidence of abortion during this time period with the end result being that most Church members likely never learned of the discrepancies in the theological approach of the animation theory but only saw that the Catholic Church vehemently opposed all abortion. On the other hand, if we saw significant evidence of the application of the animation doctrine we might surmise it was indeed considered valid. Instead, what we see is that Catholic governments prosecuted all abortions as homicide while the animation theory was still considered doctrine. Finally, the very fact that references to fetal animation could remain in Church doctrine in spite of the Pope Pius IX's decree clearly establishes that final doctrinal interpretations within the Church have depended more on leadership and/or more prominent theology as opposed to attempting to apply all doctrinal theories, conflicting at times. In the end, it is apparent the animation theory existed mostly on paper but in the whole context of applied doctrine was mostly absent and therefore irrelevant. Thus, the Catholic Church's traditional stance that all abortions were homicides stood the temporary challenge brought by the ensoulment theory and prevailed.

Nonetheless, after the Reformation the Catholic Church would lose influence in Europe and with it the door would open for attitudes regarding abortion to change, especially since its incidence would increase due to the Industrial Revolution. Eventually sexual reformers and racist Malthuisists would take up the cause of promoting the legalization of abortion in the late nineteenth and early twentieth centuries. The European sexual reformers rejected the notion of family in the traditional Christian context and promoted a world view of liberal sex so quite obviously abortion was seen as a solution to the consequences of unwanted children. The racist Malthusiasts for their part (also known as eugenists) believed in the "Malthusian Catastrophe" whereby the world's population would overtax the earth's resources at some point in the near future so abortion was seen as a viable solution to overpopulation. Also, since eugenists accepted Darwinian Evolution as fact they consequently believed the *various human races* were at various levels of evolutionary development. Therefore, given that the earth was supposedly at the limit of its ability to provide for its inhabitants it was deemed logical to check the increase in population of the "lower" races in order that the "higher" races would have less competition for the earth's resources. This was nothing more than a man-made application of *natural selection*, which is an essential feature of the theory of evolution. By the early twentieth century the racist Malthusiasts would fervently begin to promote abortion as an overpopulation solution not only for their respective countries but also for the rest of the world, and subsequently were able to influence socialists into legalizing abortion, specifically Russia and later Chile. Nonetheless, even though Russia was the first country to legalize abortion it was considered to be a temporary measure according to Lenin's commentary in "the Working Class and NeoMalthusianism". Here, Lenin severely criticized abortion and birth control measures and described them as consequences of failed capitalism due to the desperation that this system caused among the working classes.[15] Lenin did state abortion should be legalized, but taking into account his severe criticism and reference to the large numbers of illegal abortions in New York and France and it is clear Lenin believed abortion was temporarily necessary to control the high number of illegal abortions but would be phased out as communism eventually displaced capitalistic notions completely. Eventually, the well-funded eugenists used their close associations with the US government and rhetoric to influence the abortion debate in the United States and abortion would be made legal via the *Roe v. Wade* decision in 1973. Let's now look a little closer at this problematic court case.

In the *Roe v. Wade* case the high court justified the legalization abortion by referencing "apparent" international legal precedence, while ignoring others.[16] Specifically, there was a notable amount of discussion about the significance of abortion supposedly not being considered homicide before the *quickening (a.k.a. animation)*, the point the soul enters the child's body.[17] The Court also referenced a dissident Catholic historian in order to erroneously summarize the Catholic Church's historically official stance, thus enabling almost two thousand years of judicial precedence of abortion being treated as homicide to be ignored.

Furthermore, the Supreme Court also referenced the American Law Institute Model Penal Code, Tentative Draft No. 9, as an apparent justification for the legalization of abortion.[18] More precisely, this draft code had various references to very high estimates of illegal abortion in the US in the twentieth century as well as significant maternal mortality associated with the aforementioned illegal abortion estimates, which were used as a moral impetus for the legalization of abortion. All of this information was provided by sources that had long openly supported the legalization of abortion. As we shall see in a later chapter, none of these illegal abortion estimates had any real scientific methodology and none were subject to any real peer review. In fact, we shall see that these estimates were created by racist Malthusiasts in order to legalize abortion on demand and as such were nothing more than a means to an end. When considering that science had long understood that human life is created at conception, it becomes quite obvious that personal opinions were selected as a basis for the Roe v. Wade decision while history and science were thrown under the bus. One can only surmise that the court must have felt compelled to reject logic and protocol due to rising public sentiment and lobbying by abortion activists, such as Planned Parenthood and NARAL. After all this was at the height of the sexual revolution and the fervor and momentum to affirm individual rights brought about by the civil rights movement was no doubt still strong, notwithstanding the fact that in this particular case the individual right would be that of legally extinguishing the life of another person, or potential person, as was purposely crafted in the *Roe v. Wade* decision.

Therefore, it is not surprising that legal scholars call *Roe v. Wade* one of the worst decisions in the history of the US Supreme Court.[19] Here are some excerpts from law professor Mark Tushnet's opinion of *Roe v. Wade* in the Harvard Law Review:[20]

> . . . *It seems to be generally agreed that, as a matter of simple craft, Justice Blackmun's opinion for the court was dreadful* . . .

> . . . *But the conclusion that we are to draw faces two challenges: it is either uninteresting or irrelevant to constitutional theory. Insofar as Roe gives us evidence, we can conclude that Justice Blackmun is a terrible judge* . . .

In summary the Supreme Court decided to defer to propped up justifications of abortion based on an obsolete understanding of human biology as well as ignoring century's old international precedence. It also seems apparent that this verdict was the consequence of a conscious acquiescence to the abortionist lobbies at the time.

More importantly is the recognition that this decision is very weak from a legal point of view and as such would fall if challenged with sufficient vigor. The reasoning behind this observation is that the *Roe V. Wade* decision is an institutional rejection of more advanced and developed thought. It is very similar to the *Dredd Scott v. Sanford* case, and as such is in a precarious position given the dynamic prioritization of human rights. Therefore, just as in the progression of the public's conscience that the black man was fully human that eventually overturned existing obsolete laws, so too will the recognition that a human life is created at conception prompt the change in the perception of abortion, as well as its legality. There are various reasons why we can be assured of this inevitable progress toward the acceptance that abortion is homicide.

First, the scientific consensus is more concrete than ever that a unique human being is created at the moment of conception with exclusive DNA (excepting twins) due to the fact that DNA analysis has become an essential tool in science. Two of the most influential and important manifestations of this technology are genetic fingerprinting and engineering. DNA fingerprinting has become very important in the area of criminology and paternity investigations. Genetic engineering has become an important contributor to agricultural science such as increased crop yields and disease resistant plants. The discovery of DNA has made a major impact in the lives of many human beings.

Second, advances in modern medicine have allowed children to be born at earlier and earlier weeks of gestation that will eventually undermine fetal viability as a benchmark for determining a child's right to life. Also, it has been projected that in the near future an artificial womb will be created in the laboratory which expectedly would make the concept of fetal viability obsolete.

Third, we are also living in an age of information with many social media sources that are able to effectively skirt around the popular media's censorship of the facts. Thus, we can now directly challenge people to look at the actual facts of the debate.

Taking these points into account and it is clear that it is only a matter of time before legal abortion is vigorously challenged.

Abortionists groups have acknowledged this inevitable reality and not only have taken concrete steps to prevent abortion from being legally challenged but also shore up its legal precedence when it finally is challenged sufficiently. For example, since the *Roe v. Wade* decision more than 330 proposals have been submitted to Congress to recognize that a human life is created at conception, all unsuccessful of course.[21] These attempts are closely watched and tracked by multiple abortionists' groups. One specific group, the Center for Reproductive Rights, tracks attempts to propose Human Life bills in the US and Europe on their website.[22] Incredulously, the term "right to life" is consistently used on the Center for Reproductive Rights website to defend the right of a mother to kill her child and also track Human Life legislation![23] Clearly this is an attempt to re-interpret the "right to life" term in order to render it ineffective for the pro-life movement. This is further evidence that the whole abortionist movement clearly understands their success depends on not allowing any legal recognition of the beginning of human life. This is because if there was such any such recognition of the beginning of human life the "right to life" would have to be applied to the unborn child, thus causing legal abortion to fall. Therefore, it is apparent that the legal status of abortion is precarious because it depends on a legal void, specifically the absence of laws that address the beginning of human life, that could never withstand a challenge from existing Human Life Laws. As established earlier there is a nearly two thousand years of continuous juridical precedence of abortion being legally recognized as a criminal homicide due to the Catholic Church's close association with governments due to an implicit lack of separation of church and state. More recent evidence of this continuous tradition of recognizing that life begins at conception is the American Convention on Human Rights of 1969 which took place in Latin America.

Unfortunately, apparently few prolifers in the US are aware of this important fact and the positive implications it has for their cause. Similarly, for their part most Latin American pro-life groups aren't aware of the fact that Human Life legislature does not exist in the US and the advantage it brings to their cause. Rather, the focus of local campaigns seems to be to remind the population that abortion takes a human life with rarely any need to mention what science says regarding the matter, which contrasts typical North American campaigns. This may seem somewhat implausible at first, but the fact is these are Catholic majority countries whose church has a very long tradition of well over a thousand years labeling abortion as a homicide. Throw in the fact that these countries also have official agreements with the Vatican to legally prohibit abortion and mandate Christian education in public schools and it's clear to see the majority of the population is well educated in regard to when life begins. This is in spite of being regarded as having generally poorer education systems.

It is also apparent there is a coordinated effort by abortionists funded directly or indirectly by US tax dollars and the UN to muddy the issue of abortion in Latin America. Incredibly and ironically, the argument for abortion that is promoted in Latin America is a case of a *justifiable homicide* of an innocent person.

One might question the logic of a campaign that would presume to promote the *un-promotable* (the murder of a child), yet after further investigation it becomes apparent it is part of a purposeful, clever and diabolic plan. Abortionists have recognized that it would be a fruitless endeavor to convince

Latin Americans that science is not clear on the topic of when life begins. Abortionists have instead acknowledged this fact and have chosen rather to manipulate Latin American public opinion in order to create the illusion that the debate revolves around the mothers right to subordinate the right to life of their child. This is a clear case of justifiable homicide. The irony of this position should not be lost on the educated observer; specifically that abortionists in Latin America funded by US tax dollars recognize that a human life begins at birth! To put this in perspective, imagine if the current president of Planned Parenthood, Cecil Richard, announced before a packed Congress and the US public that Planned Parenthood recognizes a human child is created at birth but that the mother has the right to kill him/her!

This stance is clearly apparent in a legal opinion titled "Legal feasibility of a Technical Guide for therapeutic abortion" from the website of an abortionist NGO in Argentina directly funded by the International Planned Parenthood Federation. Below is an excerpt from the chapter titled "Uniqueness of therapeutic abortion. The right to life and integrity of women vs. conceived right":[24]

> . . . *no one negates the recognized rights of the conceived person. However, it is not justifiable to claim that these rights could threaten the life or health of a woman. In this context the decision made by the legislature, in complete agreement with the legal norms in almost all legislative bodies in the world, except in very few countries where abortion is punishable without exception, will always be in favor of prioritizing the life and health pregnant women (over the life of the conceived person).*

Here we see a misrepresentation of the facts by overtly inferring that the legal international *norm* of laws where abortion is legal is to recognize the rights of a person as a citizen at the moment of conception. Rather, in all European and North American countries where abortion on demand is legal there are no Human Life laws that recognize the new person created at the moment of conception. In fact, if there were any such laws the child's right to life would subordinate any conflicting laws, and subsequently cause the fall of legal abortion. What does exist is a legal void that purposely does not address the issue of when life begins. Conversely, Latin American countries have human life legislation and as such do not allow abortion on demand, only therapeutic abortion in some instances. However, the latter has only been made possible at the cost of millions of US tax dollars to create propaganda campaigns to convince Latin American countries that they are backwards and immoral by not legalizing therapeutic abortion. The clearly sinister efforts to legalize therapeutic abortion are not only a way to desensitize Latin Americans to the horrors of abortion, but also are being done to promote abortion as a justifiable homicide, in spite of the apparent incredibility of such a proposal.

This also calls into the question why abortionists risk acknowledging the beginning of human life at conception? One reason is to shore up their insecure position in the US and Europe due to the pro-life movements constant proposals of Human Life legislation and advances in science. Promoting the legalization of abortion in Latin America, with its existing Human Life laws in place, could be used in the future by any liberal courts in the West as legal precedent to claim that abortion is indeed compatible with Human Life laws. After all, the Supreme Court previously deferred to international precedence for the *Roe v. Wade* decision. In effect abortion would become legal even though the child's life was recognized at birth. Nonetheless, would this be sufficient justification for such a risky strategy? As we soon shall see there is a much more pressing concern which has mandated the creation of a concerted pre-emptive propaganda campaign by abortionists to prevent Latin Americans countries from realizing the significance of having Human Life legislation.

What could be this *concern* be and what are the ultimate implications? The reality is abortionists fear the revelation of never before seen information that American and Latin American pro-lifers could use to undermine the abortionist cause. In fact, the release of these facts would be so devastating to the de facto moral authority of the West that the whole infrastructure of social indicators as a means of manipulating public opinion and political negotiations would be compromised. This evidence would indeed turn the world on its end and give clear relevance to the biblical verse "the first shall be last and the last shall be first". We will see this data in a subsequent chapter but first we need to review the basis of the *moral* justification of the legalization of abortion, illegal abortion estimates.

CHAPTER THREE

A PRECURSOR TO THE ILLEGAL ABORTION DEBATE: MARGARET SANGER, PLANNED PARENTHOOD, AND THE GUTTMACHER INSTITUTE

Margaret Sanger, C.C. Little and Lothrop Stoddard founded the American Birth Control League in 1921 which eventually became Planned Parenthood Federation of America.[1] Stoddard and Little were openly racist eugenists according to the historical record. Sanger was also member of the NY Socialist Party at least from 1912, the same year that the Communist Party of the Soviet Union was founded in Russia by the Bolsheviks.[2]

Eugenics is defined "a science that tries to improve the human race by controlling which people become parents".[3] This theory is based on the notion of different human "races" which was directly derived from Darwin's theory of evolution. In fact, the term *eugenics* was coined by Francis Galton who was Charles Darwin's cousin.[4] As mentioned previously, an integral part of this theory is that the world population growth must be reduced in order to avoid a

"Malthusian Catastrophe" given that supposedly the earth would not have sufficient food for all of its inhabitants. These racist "Malthusiasts" naturally believed humans evolved from the lower animals. Furthermore, they also assumed that the *different* human *races* were at various levels of evolutionary development. Therefore, given that the earth was supposedly at the limit of its ability to provide for its inhabitants it was deemed logical to check the increase in population of the *lower races* in order that the *higher races* would have less competition for the earth's resources. This was nothing more than a manmade application of *natural selection*, which is an essential feature of the theory of evolution. With their theory *intact* the eugenists only had to decide how to implement the eradication of the *lower races*. We will see this starts by promoting birth control mostly as a tactic for changing the public's perception before promoting abortion on demand as the permanent solution.

In the article "Is Race Suicide Possible" Margaret Sanger promotes the need of controlling America's population through birth control.[5] Here is an excerpt where Sanger quotes Luther Burbank "to whom America is deeply indebted":

"America . . . is like a garden in which the gardener pays no attention to the weeds. Our criminals are our weeds, and weeds breed fast and are intensely hardy. They must be eliminated. Stop permitting criminals and weaklings to reproduce. All over the country to-day we have enormous insane asylums and similar institutions where we nourish the unfit and criminal instead of exterminating them. Nature eliminates the weeds, but we turn them into parasites and allow them to reproduce."

Here we see that *criminals* and *weaklings* are considered *weeds* which should be prevented from reproducing for the sake of society. While the term *criminals* is clear what do Sanger and other eugenists define as a *weakling*? In "Pivot of Civilization" Sanger sheds some light on this:[6]

The lack of balance between the birth rate of the "unfit" and the "fit," admittedly the greatest present menace to civilization, can never be rectified by the inauguration of a cradle competition between these two classes. The example of the inferior classes, the fertility of the feeble-minded, the mentally defective, the poverty-stricken, should not be held up for emulation to the mentally and physically fit, and therefore less fertile, parents of the educated and well-to-do classes. On the contrary, the most urgent problem to-day is how to limit and discourage the over-fertility of the mentally and physically defective. Possibly drastic and Spartan methods may be forced upon American society if it continues complacently to encourage the chance and chaotic breeding that has resulted from our stupid, cruel sentimentalism.

Therefore, Sanger held the following groups in disdain: the inferior classes, feeble-minded, mentally defective, and poverty-stricken. The definition of all but the *inferior classes* seem self-evident. In order to understand Sanger's concept of this term we need to look at Sanger's close business and ideological partners who formed the predecessor to Planned Parenthood with the stated goal of reducing the world's population, C. C. Little and Lothrop Stoddard. Stoddard had this to say in his book *The Rising Tide of Color Against White World-Supremacy:*[7]

. . . in Morocco, Central Asia, the Dutch Indies, the Philippines, and every other portion of the brown world whose inhabitants are above the grade of savages.

. . . Black Africa, as I have said, lies south of the Sahara Desert. Here the negro has dwelt for unnumbered ages. The key-note of black history, like yellow history, has been isolation. Cut off from the Mediterranean by the desert which he had no means of crossing, and bounded elsewhere by oceans which he had no skill in navigating, the black man vegetated in savage obscurity, his habitat being well named the "Dark Continent."

. . . The black man is, indeed, sharply differentiated from the other branches of mankind. His outstanding quality is superabundant animal vitality. In this he easily surpasses all other races. To it he owes his intense emotionalism. To it, again, is due his extreme fecundity, the negro being the quickest of breeders.

There can be no doubt about Stoddard perceptions regarding blacks; they were considered the most primitive of all races.

Margaret Sanger's other close associate, C.C. Little was president of the American Eugenics Society and "Third Race Betterment Conference" in 1938. Author Karen Radar offers this observation and quote of Little in *Making Mice: Standardizing Animals for American Biomedical Research, 1900-1955*:[8]

In 1926, Little had invoked what by now had become a predictable analogy to explain why the state of Maine would be a good place for doing genetics research. He described the geographical virtues of the place for sustaining humanity's pure Yankee Stock in terms similar to the ones he used to describe his animal research organisms: "I happen to be working in Maine, where the proportion of the New England stock is very, very high . . . I don't want to that particular element in this situation mixed up, or mauled up . . . "

C. C. Little makes it clear he believes the white race should be *protected* from mixing with the *lower races*. We understand this to mean Little believed the white *race* was the *pinnacle* of all human races and thus any *mixing* with the *inferior races* would have detrimental effects.

It is evident from these passages that C. C. Little and Lothrop Stoddard considered the black man to be the most inferior of all human *races* as did many eugenists. By inference we can be sure that Margaret Sanger, an avid eugenist herself, shared the same opinion or otherwise she would have not chosen them as co-founders of what is now Planned Parenthood. In fact, there is ample evidence of Sanger's racism. For example, the "Negro Project" was created to convince blacks that birth control was actually beneficial, not bothering to explain that blacks were the main focus of population control by eugenists because they were assumed to be the closest biologically relatives of the apes. Here is a quote from Sanger about "The Negro Project" in 1939:[9]

We do not want word to go out that we want to exterminate the Negro population and the minister is the man who can straighten out that idea if it ever occurs to any of their more rebellious members.

Margaret Sanger clearly took advantage of the black community's desperation to *advance* socially and economically. After all this was at the height of the depression and blacks were still severely affected by the Jim Crow laws.

Sanger's opportunism didn't stop there. She also used the discussion of birth control as a means of breaking down societies negative attitudes about abortion. While it is true Sanger spoke out against abortion (as a means of promoting the legalization of birth control) she also defended it as well, thus demonstrating her opportunistic attitude.

Here is one such example from *Woman and the New Race* written in 1920:[10]

> *Many, perhaps, will think it idle to go farther in demonstrating the immorality of large families, but since there is still an abundance of proof at hand, it may be offered for the sake of those who find difficulty in adjusting old-fashioned ideas to the facts. The most merciful thing that the large family does to one of its infant members is to kill it.*

Furthermore, given that Margaret Sanger was president when Planned Parenthood announced its efforts to legalize abortion in 1958 and it would appear that Sanger's conflicting public opinions regarding abortion were willful manipulations of public opinion.[11] There is more evidence as well of Sanger's propaganda campaign. In fact, upon closer examination of Sanger's activities and writings one can clearly see the advantages of such a deceitful plan.

Margaret Sanger was raised Catholic and thus knew the Catholic Church's historical resolve to fight birth control and abortion. She was also quite familiar with the public's attitudes towards birth control and abortion reflected in contemporary laws. After all, Sanger was indicted in 1914 for breaking postal obscenity laws by promoting birth control in her "The Women Rebel" publication and had to flee to Britain.[12] Therefore, Sanger learned very early on that in order to one day challenge abortion laws it would have to been done with the utmost discreteness.

Logically, given the opposition to birth control and abortion Sanger would have to devise a method to broach both topics. Sanger knew she was treading on legal thin ice by promoting birth control due the Comstock laws. Thus, she would need something even more shocking to make her point and give her the credibility she so desperately needed in order to challenge the status quo. Below is an excerpt from Sanger in the article "Birth Control or Abortion" from Sanger's periodical Birth Control Review in 1918:[13]

> . . . Dr. Max Hirsch, a famous authority quotes an opinion that there are 2,000,000 abortions in the United States every year. "I believe" declares Dr. Hirsch, "that I may say without exaggeration that absolutely spontaneous or unprovoked abortions are extremely rare, that a vast majority--I should estimate it at 80 per cent--have a criminal origin."

> . . . The question, then, is not whether family limitation should be practised. It is being practised; it has long been practised and it will always be practised. The question now is whether it is to be attained by normal, scientific Birth Control methods or by the abnormal, often dangerous, surgical operation.

Here we see Sanger's tactic of using the discussion of the horrors of abortion, in practice as well as magnitude, to broach the topic of birth control. Furthermore, abortion would be used as leverage in order to promote the acceptance of birth control as a *compromise solution*. Even more masterful was Sanger's discussion of the very taboo topic of abortion under the guise of its criticism. Thus, when we see Sanger's conflicting opinion's regarding abortion we can be assured it was pure opportunism nothing more, much like the Nazi's had done to drum up support among Christians through propaganda in their rise to power.

Logically, as American public opinion changed regarding the discussion of birth control and abortion so too would Sanger's strategy change. For example, by 1932 Sanger was already openly suggesting therapeutic abortion as a moral obligation.[14] Sanger was indeed pushing the boundaries of discussion with the clear objective of changing attitudes about not only birth control but also therapeutic abortion and subsequently on demand abortion.

Nevertheless, Sanger was understandably very secretive about her plan. So, while by 1932 she was resigned to suggesting the moral justification for therapeutic abortion, behind the scenes was a different story altogether. For example, two years prior Sanger planned and organized the 7th International Birth Control Conference of 1930 in Zurich, Switzerland. Here Sanger presided as president and included a session dedicated to abortion. Sanger claimed the intent of the abortion discussion was "to discuss ways to avoid abortion through the uses of better birth control".[15] However, given that the whole purpose of the conference was to promote birth control as a method of reducing unwanted pregnancies one questions the need of a special session dedicated to discussing how to reduce abortions.

Furthermore, a related conference was held in nearby Vienna a week and a half later, the Sexual Reform Congress of 1930. Sanger's the *Birth Control Review* sent a reporter to cover the conference who in turn wrote a review that clearly sympathized with the legalization of abortion:[16]

> *Birth control and illegal abortion were the subjects most stressed. Practically every speaker referred to them, and the demand for repeal of the law against abortion was general. Physicians, sociologists, poets were unanimous on this point. The physicians spoke of the danger to women of abortions performed by unskilled quacks, who are encouraged under the present law.*

As the reporter for the predecessor of Planned Parenthood noted, the topic of abortion appears to have been a prime objective of the conference. In fact, the previous Sexual Reform Conference in London passed the following resolution at the end of the conference as seen in an excerpt from Grisez's *Abortion: The Myths, the Realities, and the Arguments*:[17]

> *This Congress of the World League for Sexual Reform declares that since contraceptive methods are at present not sufficiently perfect nor widespread, many women are compelled to resort to artificial termination of pregnancy.*
>
> *In all countries except Soviet Russia this act involves severe legal penalties. These, in fact, fall mainly upon women of the poorest classes, and do not prevent the practice of abortion, but ensure that it is done secretly, incompetently, and with danger to life and health.*

We therefore call for the abolition of penalties for the mother and a revision of laws relating to abortion, so as to make it possible for a woman to obtain a termination of pregnancy by a qualified medical practitioner on economic, social, and eugenic grounds as well as the medical indications permitted at present.

It is clear the main topic of the Sexual Reform Congress conference was the legalization of abortion. In addition to sending a Birth Control Review reporter to cover the conference Sanger also sent two other persons as well, Susanna Green of Sanger's International Federation of Birth Control Leagues and E. Lester-Jones who read a report prepared by the President of Sanger's American Birth Control League, F. Robertson Jones.

So while Sanger had criticized abortion on occasion, the fact that she sent three persons to a conference dedicated to legalizing abortion is clear evidence of Sanger's deceptive tactics. Also, the following comment from the former conference demonstrates Sanger's utmost caution regarding promoting abortion before the public's attitudes had changed:[18]

This (Roman Catholic) church, although not as large as some of the Protestant sects, is strongly organized for bringing pressure to bear upon Congress and the state legislatures, and its antagonism to birth-control makes the repeal of anti-birth control laws very difficult.

While in the beginning Sanger secretly worked out of public view to change attitudes about abortion, eventually she openly started taking action to legalize abortion on demand. The first step would be to broach the topic of abortion under the guise of the criticism of high illegal abortion rates while at the same time laying the groundwork for the justification of therapeutic abortion on moral grounds to save the mother's life. Later, these same high illegal abortion rates would be used as justification of the legalization of on demand abortion under the premise that the overall rate of abortions would drop once it was legalized. The former strategy is evident below in the commentary from Dr. Frederick Taussig's (an associate or employee of Sanger's since 1928) in his book *Abortion, Spontaneous and Induced* in 1936:[19]

> *When, however, the mother is physically depleted by childbearing and poverty, when she is mentally defective or clearly irresponsible, as is the case of girls under fifteen years, in case of incest or rape, or when the mother's mental instability has reached the stage of attempted suicide we are justified I think in recommending a termination of the pregnancy.*

After having established sufficient support for the legalization of therapeutic abortion Sanger could continue to push the envelope even further to include on demand abortion. To this end Sanger helped found the International Planned Parenthood Federation in 1952[20] where three years later abortion was discussed openly at a conference in Tokyo in 1955.[21] Subsequently the Planned Parenthood Federation of America had a secret conference on abortion and in 1958 published "Abortion in the United States" which finally officially revealed PP's intent to legalize abortion in the United States.[22]

Thus, it is now clear Sanger devised a masterful plan where she would use the general repugnance of abortion to effectuate the acceptance of birth control as a compromise solution while at the same time using the opportunity to openly discuss the otherwise taboo topic of abortion. This deceptive strategy eventually desensitized the general negative perception of abortion among influential groups, thus paving the way for its future legalization. Given Sanger's early involvement with radical groups it should come as no surprise that she would abandon any sense of integrity or principal in advancing her cause of the decimation of blacks and the poor. Throw in the fact that the world was experiencing monumental change, such as women's rights to vote in the US and the growth of socialism (which was considered to be at the time a call to increasing recognition of the individual's rights), Sanger must have felt the momentum for *change* to be compelling. It is clear Sanger was a true opportunist who would do and say anything to advance her cause to depopulate the world starting with the *lower races* first.

Not conspicuously, Sanger had a contemporary who used similar tactics of deception and pseudoscience to break down social barriers for the eugenist agenda; Adolf Hitler. In fact, it turns out that the American eugenist movement was by some accounts the justification that the Nazi's chose to create their *final solution*. After all Hitler used the same tactics and justification of racial genocide that Sanger employed for his own particular version, the Holocaust.

Evidence of the Sanger-Hitler connection is offered by noted Jewish American author:[23]

> . . . *Hitler studied American eugenics laws. He tried to legitimize his anti-Semitism by medicalizing it, and wrapping it in the more palatable pseudoscientific facade of eugenics. Hitler was able to recruit more followers among*

reasonable Germans by claiming that science was on his side. Hitler's race hatred sprung from his own mind, but the intellectual outlines of the eugenics Hitler adopted in 1924 were made in America . . .

. . . Hitler proudly told his comrades just how closely he followed the progress of the American eugenics movement. "I have studied with great interest," he told a fellow Nazi, "the laws of several American states concerning prevention of reproduction by people whose progeny would, in all probability, be of no value or be injurious to the racial stock."

To continue, Hitler and Sanger's *final solutions* from the beginning were to rid their societies of unwanted *races* but they also understood any attempt would be resisted fiercely by Christian groups, especially the well-organized Catholics. Therefore, it was deemed of utmost importance to endear themselves to their respective audiences first while gradually desensitizing the population. To this end Hitler and Sanger would gradually substitute Christian notions as a moral basis for society with nationalism and individual rights, respectively. Both plans were carried out with the utmost diabolical precision and deceit and consequently have left a wound on the world that has yet to heal.

The smoke and mirrors tactics of Planned Parenthood didn't stop with Sanger's departure in 1962, but continued with its new president, Alan Guttmacher. Guttmacher, for his own part, was equally unprincipled and motivated by racism to justify the elimination of the *lesser races* by deceit and coercion. Planned Parenthood created the Center for Family Planning

Program Development to be run by Guttmacher. Eventually, the Center was renamed the Guttmacher Institute.

The 1960's was a period great change spurred on by many factors, such as the civil rights movement, the Vietnam War, the sexual revolution, and real time world news. The diffusion of information and opinion was enabled by the widespread proliferation of television and radios. The popular news media soon began to take on the role as a proxy moral authority that would call attention to unjust governments while also promoting causes. The world was entering an unprecedented era of expectation for positive change.

Nonetheless, in spite of this overwhelming feeling of hope due to the fall of racial barriers, Alan Guttmacher stays true to the racist precepts of Planned Parenthoods founders. Guttmacher accomplishes this by targeting the *lower races* for elimination by reducing their birth rates, by deception or coercion as needed. This is evident in the following quote from an interview in 1970:[24]

> *If the United States goes to the black man or the yellow man and says slow down your reproductive rate, we're immediately suspected of having ulterior motives to keep the white man dominant in the world. If you send in a colorful UN force, you've got much better leverage.*

Given the fact that Guttmacher made this statement six years after the Civil Rights Act of 1964 it should be clear Guttmacher had a deeply racist perspective of the world. As further evidence of this Neanderthalic attitude, Guttmacher made a similar statement just one year before in an article titled "Family Planning, The Needs and Methods,"[25]

Some type of population control is inevitable if civilization is to survive. The great problem is whether it can be done voluntarily or whether it must be done through coercion. We hope it can be on a voluntary basis.

Some people say a maximum family size should be established. I am not yet of that opinion. I would like to give our voluntary means of population control full opportunity in the next 10 or 12 years. Then, if these don't succeed, we may have to go into some kind of coercion, not worldwide, but possibly in places as India, Pakistan, and Indonesia where pressures are great.

Notice that Guttmacher focused his devious attention on the *lesser races* as did all his other racist predecessors of Planned Parenthood. It is also apparent Guttmacher would use the same tactics that made Margaret Sanger infamous via "the Negro Project" but would even take it a step further by promoting birth control by coercion.

Incredibly, it seems that Guttmacher could propose such openly racist opinions and not be tarred in feathered in the public forums. One must remember that the late 1960s were still a period of transition in the US, where institutional and other forms of racism were gradually being discredited. Nonetheless, such inflammatory remarks would seem to have drawn the attention of the black community. Indeed, the more volatile elements such as Jesse Jackson and the Black Muslims spoke out against Planned Parenthood[26] after having witnessed firsthand the devastating effects of the "Negro Project". Undoubtedly this was due to the significant reduction of the black population and detrimental effects on the black family, but apart from that, it appears Guttmacher's statements flew under the radar. One might question why Jesse Jackson, the Black Muslims, and others like the Black Panthers vocal opposition failed to generate substantial resistance to Planned Parenthood. Nonetheless, looking at the particular situation of blacks prior to this period and the answer is clear.

Blacks in the US after emancipation were legally and emotionally oppressed by the Democrat Party's Jim Crow laws and the Ku Klux Klan. Sanger clearly recognized this desperation in the black community and used this knowledge to create her nefarious "The Negro Project." After all, the level of frustration and disassociation from American society of the average black individual would have made almost any proposition that would "increase" the overall wealth and thus importance of the black community seem like a dream come true. One could surmise that Sanger, ever the skilled orator and writer, was able to convince the desperate black community leaders that limiting to a significant extent the number of their children was necessary in order that the black community could *take charge* of their lives. No doubt Sanger did not take the time to explain that birth control would eventually cause the black population to fall and with it the black community's future political relevance. Instead, she explained to them that fewer children meant a better standard of living for the family.[27] In fact, Sanger's ability to convince the black community to willingly destroy itself from within speaks to her effectiveness as a compelling communicator that rivals her contemporary and partner in racial cleansing, Adolf Hitler.

There is more evidence that demonstrates the black community was more than eager to embrace change to improve their condition during this time period. In the presidential election of 1936 the Democrat candidate Roosevelt was able to garner a large number of black votes from the Republican Party of Lincoln, in spite of the Democrat Party's overtly racist past. This was during the midst of the Great Depression where large amounts of Americans were suffering, especially blacks, and undoubtedly Roosevelt's New Deal was seen as a lifeline for blacks who had up until this point in history had been mostly ignored by the US government. Black's were clearly desperate at this point in time and Margaret Sanger would take do her best to take advantage of the situation. Of notable importance is the fact that from this point on the Democrat Party gradually increased its proportion of the black vote until the Civil Rights Act of 1964 was signed in to law by the Democratic President, Lyndon Johnson, whereupon it has maintained a level of over 90 percent.[28]

Martin Luther King's apparent support of Planned Parenthood would have certainly influenced black opinion (based on the fact that he accepted an award from Planned Parenthood in 1966) and enabled Planned Parenthood's targeting of the black community for extinction to be all but ignored.[29] More evidence of the black community's desperate desire for relevance was Jesse Jackson's complete about face on the issue of abortion, something he once called a " genocide,"[30] out of apparent political necessity after the Democratic Party embraced abortion as a party platform in 1976.[31] Undoubtedly Jackson, like some in the black community who embraced Sanger's "the Negro Project," believed the sacrifice of the black family and/or black children was an equitable exchange for increasing black affluence and for Jackson's particular case, increased participation in politics.

While the issue of the *black genocide* was relegated to the *back burner* in the early 1970s, it quickly became a non-issue within the black community given that the Democratic Party adopted abortion as a party platform. As such, any criticism of the largest provider of abortion in the US, Planned Parenthood, would be squashed out of political necessity. This enabled Guttmacher to emerge unscathed by the newly wrought politically correct machine that was the US *free* press, thus ensuring a more or less *benevolent* historical perception.

In summary, the eugenist and racist founders of Planned Parenthood believed that the earth's resources could not support additional population growth and therefore a plan would need to be implemented to reduce the world's population, first by birth control and later abortion. Since Eugenics theory is firmly founded on the principles of Darwinism Evolution it was taken as fact that *human races* evolved from the lower animals and as such the various *races* were at different levels of evolutionary progress. Therefore, it was only logical to focus most energy on eliminating the *lower races* by targeting their birth rates as a solution to overpopulation. Naturally, the Northern European eugenists considered blacks to be the least evolutionary developed, not far removed from the apes. Margaret Sanger devised a sinister strategy of promoting the *moral necessity* of birth control to break down barriers to therapeutic abortion while Guttmacher used a similar strategy to break down the resistance to abortion on demand. We see that deception was essential to this plan given that the *lesser races* would not willingly allow themselves to be eliminated. In fact, the evidence of this plan is apparent today where Planned Parenthood has 79 percent of its abortion facilities located within walking distance of minority neighborhoods.[32] The *fruits* of this plan are that blacks are five times more likely to have abortion than whites.[33] Also, Sanger's prolific propaganda was very effective in garnering support for racial targeting, just as her eugenist counterpart the Nazi Party had done in Germany. We will see in the following chapters that this disregard of science continues to be a major modus operandi of Planned Parenthood and its derivative in charge of propaganda, the Guttmacher Institute.

CHAPTER FOUR

COMPROMISED SCIENCE: INSTITUTIONALIZED BIAS IN SCIENTIFIC RESEARCH

"Social indicators" is demographic information that is used to characterize and/or quantify for the purpose of comparison. For example, if the object of the social indicators is a region this could be used be determine how this particular region compares to others in terms of economic wealth, crime, health, mortality, and so forth.

> . . . the purpose of the SSDS is to show what data are desirable on human beings, both individual and in groups, and on the institutions with which they are connected and how these data should be organized in order to provide an information system which will be useful for description, analysis and policy making in the different fields of social life.

Many governments, international organizations and non-governmental organizations use this information in order direct and justify policy and legislative decisions. The United

Nations, World Bank, and WHO have statistics available to governments, NGO's, and the public.[3, 4, 5]

While social indicators have become an essential tool for governments in the last half century, demographic analysis has been used in various forms back to antiquity, specifically the population census. The ancient Greeks, Romans, and Israelites all used such studies to count its citizens. Also, the Roman Catholic Church expanded on this concept and has long kept a record of births, deaths, and marriages which was subsequently continued by Protestant denominations.

With the rise of secularism in Europe due to the Reformation, philosophers and scientists became interested in applying reason and science to resolve societal problems as opposed to mostly a religious perspective promoted by the Roman Catholic Church. Cartesianism and the Enlightenment played major roles in the development of the concept of social science as a means of improving society.[6] This theme was further developed during the Enlightenment. Subsequently Malthusianism and its dependent Eugenics utilized certain social indicators for the justification of the implementation of their depopulation schemes.

In 1639 Massachusetts became the first American colony to require the record keeping of all births, marriages, and deaths.[7] After the formation of the United States of America a census was taken at ten year intervals. Initially, the census counted the number of persons but during the nineteenth century additional categories were added to include information about mortality, manufacturing, agriculture, etc. By 1870 the categories of "social statistics" and "vital statistics" were added, including births and deaths, although incomplete.[8] By 1900 homicides had been added and by 1929 abortions were included as well.[9, 10] In 1930 crime statistics were issued by the Federal Bureau of Investigation.[11] The United Kingdom has kept detailed statistics of crime of England and Wales since 1898 and public records show crime statistics have been kept since 1800.[12, 13]

Only relatively recently have social indicators taken on considerable importance in policy making decisions and consequently acted as an impetus for the justification of allotment of substantial amounts of public money. Some common examples are the US governments' tracking of unemployment, interest rates, disease, education standards, crime, etc. Understandably the US has derived many tangible benefits from properly executed statistical analysis. Adjusting the prime interest rate in response to low employment rates in order to stimulate economic growth is a relevant example. Unfortunately, social indicator studies are also subject to political interest, greed, and corruption where it would then be relegated to nothing more than pseudo-scholarly propaganda used to promote political agendas. The consequences of misusing such a powerful analytical tool have resulted in far reaching implications as we shall see.

One might question how is it possible that *science* and *disinterested* professionals could be manipulated in order that the *results* of demographic studies end up with a predictable *outcome*. However, when one takes the time to look at the various factors involved in research the inherent fragility becomes apparent.

Science as the term is generally used by the public today has become to mean the *accepted* theories of an academic discipline(s). *Theories* are supposed to be well deliberated ideas that attempt to explain, mimic, and/or predict natural phenomena and have a basis in empirical evidence or mathematical models. Theories are often based on the results of controlled observations where proposed parameters are isolated in order to determine a cause and effect relationship. Not all proposed theories can be readily proven if at all due to various factors such as lack of available data of the phenomenon in question.

New theories are constantly being published by the research community, which is comprised of many universities, private, and public institutions around the world. However, before these new theories are widely accepted they must pass a process of review by other professionals in the same field(s). Theories are generally considered *temporary* until superseded by another that has been deemed through peer review to be more complete or accurate. The preparation of any study should entail the participation of professionals with expertise in the field in question and since research proposals generally originate with or involve the collaboration of scientists this is not an issue. In the event research involves various interdisciplinary variables it would seem logical that the research team would have to include all of the disciplines that could possibly be involved. Conversely, the absence of involvement by qualified professionals in the elaboration of a scientific study could have the result that any proposed theories would likely be of low academic merit due to an incomplete understanding of the phenomenon that is being analyzed. Obviously, any proposed theory based on flawed methodology could have severe consequences depending on how said information is used, such as a justification of public policy or laws. Normally, the process of peer review would discredit any unsound theories due to flawed methodology or other issues. Nonetheless, in the event that for whatever reason a theory goes unchallenged, i.e. it is not subject to the peer review process, it would then by default become the *accepted* theory in the particular field that it is applied, whether flawed or not.

Currently, most of the research and development funding in the US originates from industry and government sources and accounts for $436 billion in gross expenditures which is about 2.9 percent of the GDP.[14] Eighteen US corporations are among the fifty top global companies in research and development spending which suggests public companies are the major source of funding from industry.[15]

According to the Human Rights Campaign Foundation of the top US manufacturers all but three have a "Corporate Equality Index" of ninety or more on a scale of one hundred.[16, 17] This index is a measure of a company's support of LGBT policies. Given that more Americans than ever before support homosexual marriage[18] and that public companies live and die by public perception it is quite understandable that the management of publicly traded companies take public trends and opinions very seriously. After all few publically traded companies would knowingly risk funding a project that would hurt their perception in the public eye because of a consequential drop in stock prices as a *knee-jerk* reaction to unpopular policies.

In the same vein, government entities would not be interested in funding politically charged topics because of the danger of reduced funding for their departments in the next fiscal cycle. This is due to the fact that politicians approve government budgets and when a re-election is at stake, few are willing to go against public opinion and fund unpopular research. Also, any appointed government official that chooses to go *against the grain* and fund politically sensitive research runs the risk of being replaced for putting his sponsor's political career in jeopardy.

In summary, research and development is big business and is driven mostly by public companies and government entities which are very sensitive to public opinion. This, in turn, has the effect of limiting research topics for which funds are available. This sensitivity to *problematic* topics also can influence the peer review process as well. This is due to the fact that any scientist that publicly criticizes a topic that has been embraced by the public runs the risk of being professionally ostracized. The effects of research being driven by sponsors who in turn are beholden to public opinion has created an inherent bias in scientific research and investigation. The result is that the majority of available funding is for *preferred* research topics only. It turns out research for topics concerning abortion, such as illegal abortion estimates, have long been ignored by the academic community. This has allowed a very small group to control the illegal abortion estimate debate, in spite of the fact these same groups were all created to legalize abortion.

In the following chapter, we will look specifically at the case of illegal abortion estimates as a social indicator. Here we will see the consequences of the scientific community's unwillingness to to fund research critical of abortion that has allowed illegal abortion estimates to be all but exempt from peer review for decades, enabling this flawed theory to go virtually unchallenged and effect large scale public policies that are equally without merit, but in fact will have devastating long term effects.

CHAPTER FIVE

COMPROMISED SCIENCE: TRADITIONAL ESTIMATES OF ILLEGAL ABORTION INCIDENCE

Surprisingly, even as statistics of crime were compiled in the early twentieth century in the US and Europe, abortion was still deemed as *very difficult* to quantify even up until to the *Roe v. Wade* decision. Not conspicuously the primary source of illegal abortion estimates, the Guttmacher Institute, was also a proponent of birth control and legal abortion. Thus it is evident there was a clear conflict of interests. Furthermore, these same illegal abortion estimates have virtually remained unchallenged to this day and subsequently have become the primary justification for the United States' and United Nations' public policy of promoting the legalization of abortion. In the previous chapter, we saw the political direction that research has taken which effectively precludes research of sensitive topics, such as illegal abortion estimates. Nonetheless, this isn't the only reason that has enabled the Guttmacher Institute estimates from being subjected to serious peer review. Let's now take a look at these figures from its earliest recorded incidences up until the present day in order to reveal other factors that allowed illegal abortion estimates by the Malthusiasts at the Guttmacher Institute to be insulated from other demographic indicators.

One of the earliest estimates of the period that appears in literature is from an article in the periodical "Medical Record, a journal of medicine and surgery" in 1893. Here is an excerpt:[1]

The Number of criminal Abortions in this city was very great during January and February. The opinion has been expressed that only one in every thousand cases are detected. At this rate the number in New York would be about eighty thousand a year. Some astute gentleman has emitted the theory that there has been an increase in criminal abortion because the police have been compelled by force of public opinion to look a little more sharply into the number and character of the city's brothels!

Here we see an estimate of 80,000 abortions a year for New York City in 1893. Lacking any descriptive methodology, we are obliged to infer that the number of abortions is based on anecdotal evidence derived from casual observation. Furthermore, a multiplying factor of some sort has been added to the final tally as evidenced by the statement that "only 1 in 1000 cases of abortion are "detected". No justification for this inflationary factor is offered either so this must be attributed to speculation. Given that the composite total is derived in part from casual observation and speculation the only logical conclusion is that the figure of 80,000 abortions is of limited scholarly value.

Nonetheless, in spite of the weakness of this estimate it would appear it formed the basis for an illegal abortion projection for the whole of the US. Specifically, a figure of two million abortions appears in literature of the period and has been referenced in numerous other publications up until fairly recently and even has been considered to be "authoritative." For example, in Margaret Sanger's *The Case for Birth Control* in 1917 she includes an excerpt by Dr. Max Hirsch who cites the same estimates for New York City from the *Medical Record* and its apparent projected incidence over the whole US population:[2]

> *According to a report in the Medical Record 80,000 abortions are performed annually in New York and only one case in 1,000 is brought before the authorities.*

> *According to Lewin it has been determined by court investigations that there are at least 200 people in New York who make a profession of performing abortions.*

> *It has been estimated that 2,000,000 abortions are performed annually in the U. S.*

Sanger would continue to reference Max Hirsch as an authority of illegal abortion estimates. Not so conspicuously Hirsch was a prominent German eugenist who was also an important member of the "Society of Physicians for Sexology and Eugenics".[3] According to the introduction of the "6th World Congress of Sexology" the discipline of sexology arose in the nineteenth century from various factors:[4]

> *In the 19th century, new concerns about overpopulation, sexual psychopathy and degeneracy gave rise to the concept of "sexuality" and led to intensified efforts on many fronts to get a firmer intellectual grasp on a subject matter that*

rapidly seemed to grow ever more complex. Biological, medical, historical, and anthropological research by von Baer, Darwin, Mendel, Kaan, Morel, Magnan, Charcot, Westphal, Burton, Morgan, Mantegazza, Westermarck, Krafft-Ebing, Schrenck-Notzing, and others, laid the foundations of sex research in the modern, more specific sense. Finally, at the turn of the 20th century, the pioneering work of Havelock Ellis, Sigmund Freud, and Iwan Bloch established the investigation of sexual problems as a legitimate endeavor in its own right.

Sexology, like Eugenics, is intimately linked to the issue of overpopulation. Furthermore, after more than a century of evidence of the results of *sexology* and other related movements, it is clear another prime objective was to expand the acceptable norms of sexual behavior to include promoting promiscuous behavior. To this end, as societies concepts of sexual relations gradually became increasingly separated from the concept of marriage it naturally would require the promotion of birth control (and later abortion) as a means to prevent the unnecessary consequences of a child. Within this context, when we see Margaret Sanger referencing Dr. Hirsch's illegal abortion estimates of two million in 1918 it is only reasonable to question the validity of such figures given that sexology has the very same ideological impetus to promote birth control and abortion as did eugenics.

Sanger continues to reference similar *estimates* of illegal abortion by other persons involved in the same cause as her – to promote birth control initially while using high illegal abortion rates as a scare tactic. For example, in her periodical *Birth Control Review* in 1918 Sanger states:[5]

In the very nature of the case, it is impossible to get accurate figures upon the number of abortions performed annually in the United States. It is often said, however, that one in five pregnancies end in abortion. One estimate is that 150,000 occur in the United States each year and that 25,000 women die of the effects of such operations in every twelve months. Dr. William J. Robinson asserts that there are 1,000,000 abortions every year in this country and adds that the estimate is conservative. He quotes Justice John Proctor Clark as saying that there are at least 100,000 in the same length of time in New York City alone.

Interestingly enough we see this estimate introduces figures of maternal mortality, which shortly thereafter would become a permanent feature of the argument for legal abortion. Faced with the reality that maternal mortality is still an essential impetus behind the moral imperative for the legalization of abortion and it should be clear the seemingly inconspicuous inclusion of maternal mortality figures at this point in time was not by chance, but was instead part of a carefully thought out plan. Maternal mortality rates along with illegal abortion would be introduced as the moral framework for the argument to legalize abortion while it was still very much a taboo topic. As we noted previously Sanger's constant reference of illegal abortion estimates was used as leverage to promote birth control as well, thus starting a dialogue which would later be meticulously expanded to include the proposed eventual outright promotion of the legalization of abortion in the US.

The author of the aforementioned illegal abortion estimate, Dr. William Robinson, was another racist Malthusiast and thus advocate of birth control as well and a colleague or business partner of Margaret Sanger given that she at one point considered giving Dr. Robinson her cherished *Birth Control Review*.[6] Not surprisingly, there is no real methodology for Robinson's figures which obligates us to assume it is based on anecdotal observation. Dr. Robinson would later publish "The Law Against Abortion: Its Perniciousness Demonstrated and Its Repeal Demanded" whose stated goal is obvious enough.[7]

In 1933 Dr. A. J. Rongy, a fellow racist Malthusiast in New York City like Sanger, published a work titled "Abortion: Legal or Illegal?" that attempted to push the envelope of the discussion of legalizing abortion. Here Dr. Rongy estimates 2,000,000 illegal abortions in the US.[8] Shortly after, in 1935 Sanger references an estimate of 800,000 illegal abortions by a *conservative investigator* Dr. Frederick Taussig.[9] Dr. Taussig was a colleague of Sanger's and member of Sanger's "National Committee on Federal Legislation on Birth Control" who would go on to publish an estimate of 681,600 illegal abortions in 1936 in *Spontaneous and Induced: Medical and Social Aspects* which also promoted the legalization of abortion.[10] Remembering that Sanger sent various representatives to an abortion conference in Vienna and the fact that Taussing appeared frequently in the *Birth Control Review* as well as being a member of National Committee on Federal Legislation on Birth Control and one should suspect that Sanger was promoting abortion by proxy through Taussig. Again, this was long before she supposedly *officially* supported legal abortion in the 1950s.

Dr. Taussig's estimate along with other subsequent estimates from later years are referenced by the American Law Institute Model Penal Code, Tentative Draft No. 9, which was used in the Supreme Court's *Roe v. Wade* decision. This is significant because it was more than likely considered to be relevant information for the final court opinion.[11] The following table lists commonly reported illegal abortion estimates in the US, some of which were also referenced in the *Roe v. Wade* decision.

TABLE 1 - ILLEGAL ABORTION ESTIMATES

Year	Region	Abortions	Source
1893	NYC	80,000	Medical Record
1914	US	2,000,000	Hirsch
1916	US	1,000,000	Robinson
1933	US	2,000,000	Rongy
1935	US	800,000	Taussig - Sanger
1936	US	681,600	Taussig
1944	US	332,329	Dunn
1944	US	415,000	Whelpton
1958	US	1,200,000	Calderone

Based on the differing populations and widely varying illegal abortion estimates it would be natural to suspect the estimation methodology was never formulated adequately. Nonetheless, instead of resolving the issue of the unscientific methods of estimation it apparently appeared more fortuitous to establish that abortion has *inherent* estimation difficulties. Not so conspicuously this often-repeated claim continues to this day in that the Guttmacher Institute claims illegal abortion incidence is difficult to quantify. Nonetheless, this apparent *fact* has not stopped the Guttmacher Institute and other pro-abortion groups from attempting to do that which they claim is practically impossible and then ironically lobbying for said estimates to be used as a basis for setting public policy. Taking this into account and the fact that seven out of the nine sources of illegal abortion estimates in Table 1 were proponents for the legalization of abortion and a very clear picture develops of the protagonists of said estimates utilizing their *studies* and ample promotional and organizational resources to establish themselves as the undisputed authorities in a field virtually devoid of competition. All of this was made possible by apparently ample funding by the Rockefellers (based by the number of organizations Sanger managed as well as the professional members and frequent conferences). Later, with the *Roe v. Wade* decision and the new found support of the liberal press and politicians and the stage was set for these groups to become even more entrenched as they were able to not only rely on their plentiful private funding but now had public funds as well. Coupled with a considerable amount of public support, they were assured there would be practically no private or public funding for dissenting estimates.

As mentioned previously, when abortion started to draw the attention of the newly formed medical professions the incidences of illegal abortion were being directly inferred from either the mere mention of abortion among physicians in literature or from observations lacking any real formulated methodology. This type of *evidence* is classified as anecdotal and thus considered to be of low value. Surprisingly and unfortunately this unsound processes of associating the incidence of an event with its mention in historical literature is still used quite frequently in books and opinion articles regarding the topic of historical abortion. The result of these often-repeated defective opinions combined with numerous non-peer reviewed illegal abortion estimates has created a seamless and apparent bulletproof concept of induced abortion as a significant and even *natural* feature of the human experience.

However, in spite of assertions that published illegal abortion rates are valid (by groups that have an ideological impetus to promote abortion) there is ample evidence that this is not the case, in fact. We will review this evidence and offer a new methodology based on an existing scientific discipline. Before getting started, it will be necessary to briefly discuss some common terminology and their origins. Also, a standard will need to be established in order to serve as a basis of comparison of published abortion figures with our soon to be proposed rates.

As mentioned in the previous chapter, one of the earlier abortion estimates appeared in the latter part of the nineteenth century in the *Medical Record*. Here an abortion rate was derived from the observation of an area of notably high prostitution and applied over the population of New York City for a total 80,000 annual abortions.[12] Subsequently, some twenty years later Hirsch proposed a figure of two million abortions for the whole of the United States. This is one of the first examples of an overall annual figure of illegal abortion for the US. This is significant because a rate of incidence would have been preferable because it would have enabled the comparison of estimates of widely differing populations. Nonetheless, given that Hirsch's goal as a eugenist was to reduce the world's population at all costs (in order to prevent the *inevitable Malthusian catastrophe*) it can be surmised that the overall abortion figure was purposely presented as a total for its shock value. In fact, the inclusion of total abortion figures was one of Margaret Sanger's primary propaganda tactics that appear constantly in her writings and speeches.

By the 1930's eugenists would begin to relate abortion to live births and high maternal mortality rates. For example, in 1936 Sanger's colleague Taussig would propose a ratio of abortions to live births in his book *Abortion. Spontaneous and Induced: Medical and Social Aspects*.[13] Sanger herself in the following year would make claims that 25 percent of annual maternal mortality was directly caused by illegal induced abortion.[14] This is significant because now abortion would begin to be related exclusively to women's health and childbirth and thus would serve to isolate abortion from other social indicators even though abortion was already being classified using the standard rate per 100,000 population by the US Bureau of the Census.[15]

Not surprisingly, by 1946 "abortion" as a term was replaced by "stillbirth" in the US Census' "Vital Statistics Reports of the United States".[16] Also of considerable importance is the fact that now stillbirth rates were published as a percentage of live births in official government publications, which is exactly what Taussig did ten years earlier, thus doing away completely with the standard rate per 100,000 population.

It is relevant to note that the changes to the way abortion was officially reported happened under Halbert Dunn, who only two years prior in 1944 presented illegal abortion figures at a conference held by the National Committee on Maternal Health "NCMH", an organization that worked closely with Margaret Sanger. The NCMH was funded at the time by Rockefeller (who also funded Margaret Sanger) and eventually would become the Population Council, which the Guttmacher Institute (a derivative of Sanger's Planned Parenthood) references for illegal abortion estimates.[17] Also, Dunn's estimates by all accounts influenced the *Roe v. Wade* decision per the Supreme Courts reference to the Model Penal Code.[18, 19] Interestingly enough, it appears Halbert Dunn was a member of the Unitarian Universalist Church.[20] This is significant because the Unitarian Church leadership had long been outspoken supporters of birth control and worked closely with Margaret Sanger and would later support the legalization of abortion on demand in 1968.[21, 22] Taking into account Sanger's manipulation of the early abortion debate and Dunn's close association with eugenists, the significant change in the official US government reporting of abortion suggests a purposeful effort to isolate abortion from other social indicators, something eugenists long strived to obtain.

After the legalization of abortion in the US rates of occurrence of abortion were beginning to be offered in terms of *abortion rate* and *abortion ratio*. The abortion rate is defined as the number of abortions per 1000 women of reproductive age. The abortion ratio is defined as the number of abortions per 100 live births. This is important because these methods of quantification only further isolated abortion as a social issue, thus making equitable comparisons to other demographic indicators that much more difficult.

In summary, the historical record demonstrates that abortion rates were initially related to the overall population (a logical and common practice). Nonetheless, after apparent influence by eugenists, abortion would begin to be related exclusively to birth and women's issues, such as maternal mortality, births, and women's population. Understanding Sanger's goal of *empowering* women and this manipulated separation of abortion from any connection to the overall population was logically necessary in order that abortion would become exclusive to women's issues. This practice of quantifying abortion continues to this day. For example, all the primary sources of illegal abortion estimates use this methodology to include the Guttmacher Institute, all US governmental agencies as well as the United Nations, and international NGO's. Thus, it seems apparent the ultimate goal was to present the legalization of abortion as a *human rights* issue, as abortion is now promoted.

Now that we have reviewed the history of the illegal abortion debate the next step will be to present *traditional* abortion estimates using standard methodology that is currently used by many US governmental and United Nations agencies for all types of demographics analysis. This is the very same method that was initially utilized by the US Census Bureau to report abortion before being changed some fifteen years later after its inception.

In demographics, one of the most common ways to infer a phenomenon's impact on a particular society is to compare the rate of occurrence of said phenomenon with that of other societies. A major advantage of this method is that the size of the population is generally not important with the result being equitable comparisons that can be made between diverse countries. In fact, the UN and the World Bank offer many of their compiled social indicators in this same format. Some examples are birth rates and homicides. The rate of occurrence (or incidence) is calculated by dividing the number of occurrences in a given time period by the population and then multiplying the resultant by 100,000. This is demonstrated in the following formula:

FIGURE 1 - RATE OF OCCURRENCE FORMULA

$$\frac{n}{P} \times 100{,}000 = r = \text{"rate of occurrence/incidence"}$$

n = occurrences
P = population

Generally, but not always, the time period is one year. Also, the calculated rate is only representative of the population used in the calculation, which could be a geographic region or a characteristic, such as sex or age. In the above equation, the *rate of occurrence* of the event in question is per a population of 100,000 persons.

Previously, we presented some commonly referenced illegal abortion estimates in the US prior to the *Roe v. Wade* decision. Now let's see these same figures in terms of the international demographic standard as seen above in figure 1:

TABLE 2 - POPULATION ABORTION RATES

Year	Population Region	Year of Census	Population (millions)	Abortions	Population Abor. Rate	Source
1893	NYC	1890	1.515	80,000	5,281	Medical Record
1914	US	1910	92.407	2,000,000	2,164	Hirsch
1916	US	1910	92.407	1,000,000	1,082	Robinson
1933	US	1930	123.076	2,000,000	1,625	Rongy
1935	US	1930	123.076	800,000	650	Taussig - Sanger
1936	US	1930	123.076	681,600	554	Taussig
1944	US	1940	132.122	332,329	252	Dunn
1944	US	1940	132.122	415,000	314	Whelpton
1958	US	1950	152.271	1,200,000	788	Calderone
1970	US	1970	205.052	1,000,000	488	NARAL

The term "Population Abortion Rate" as shown in Table 2 is the annual rate of abortions for the regions shown for a population of 100,000 inhabitants. The "Year of the Census" represents the population data from most previous census data prior to the published date of the estimate, "year". Using this common method, it is apparent that there was a great deal of discrepancy between published estimated illegal population abortion rates even up to only a few short years before the *Roe v. Wade* decision.

Now let's look at more current legal and illegal abortion ratios published by the Guttmacher Institute and frequently cited as an *authoritative* source by the United Nations, WHO, the European Union, and the US:[23]

TABLE 3 - PUBLISHED ABORTION RATIOS

	Abortion Ratio		
	Total	Safe	Unsafe
World	32	16	16
Developed countries*	44	41	3
Excluding Eastern Europe	30	30	0
Developing countries*	31	14	17
Excluding China	27	7	20
Africa	18	1	17
Asia	35	21	14
Europe	54	50	5
Latin America	41	2	39
Northern America	29	29	0
Oceania	21	18	3

In Table 3 the lowest reported total incidence of abortion is 16 per 100 live births. The clear implication is that there is a *base* abortion rate common to all countries that apparently is not influenced by beliefs or customs. Also, conspicuously the countries with among the highest percentages of Catholics (Latin America) also supposedly have among the highest incidences of abortion in spite of the fact that these same countries have Christian education mandated by official agreement with the Vatican. Obviously, this seems completely out of place given that for almost two thousand years the Catholic Church has been teaching life begins at conception and as such abortion is a serious sin and thus prohibited. In fact, to demonstrate the effect of this education (as mentioned in chapters three and six) abortionists have resigned themselves to promoting abortion as a legal homicide in Latin American due to the local population's clear understanding of the topic of abortion.

As mentioned earlier, the abortion ratio is a measure of abortion per live births. This measurement is very commonly seen and understandably is an effective method of associating abortion to an event exclusive to women, specifically childbirth, thus disassociating it from other demographic indicators not only conceptually but also pragmatically in that comparisons with many other indicators are inhibited. In fact, without having live birth data there is no simple method of conversion from the abortion ratio to the standard rate per 100,000 population.

Nonetheless, there is another commonly used figure, specifically the "abortion rate", which can be more readily converted to the demographic standard of incidence. This method is similar to the abortion ratio in that the basis of measurement, in this case the number of fertile women, is tied to a characteristic exclusive to women. The abortion rate calculation depends on the number of fertile women in a population, which generally is determined to be the age range of fifteen to forty-four or forty-nine years, depending on the source. While the number of fertile women is not published, generally this can be derived using total abortion figures and rates. Then, combined with total population figures an estimate of the percentage of fertile women in any given population can be calculated. There is some error involved but the coefficient of variation is quite low for our sampling of 30 countries (0.10). Thus, for purposes of conversion of abortion rates to a total incidence in the population, we will assume the percentage of fertile women in any given population is 22 percent. Therefore, the conversion from the often published "abortion rate", "AR_e", to the "population abortion rate" "PAR" is:

FIGURE 2 - DERIVATION OF PAR FROM ABORTION RATE

$$PAR = ARe \times 0.22 \times 100$$

Below is a table of published Unsafe Abortion Rates for 2008 converted to the Population Abortion Rate (original figures provided by the Guttmacher Institute via the World Health Organization):[24]

TABLE 4 - COMPARISON OF PUBLISHED ABORTION RATES TO CORRESPONDING "PAR"

	Unsafe Abortion Rate	Population Abor. Rate
World	14	308
Developed countries	1	22
Developing countries	16	352
Least devel. countries	27	594
Sub-Sahara Africa	31	682
Africa	28	616
Asia	11	242
Europe	2	44
Latin America	31	682
Northern America	0	0
Oceania	8	176

Interestingly, the illegal abortion estimates in Table 4 don't differ to a great degree from the values offered by eugenists after 1935 up until the *Roe v. Wade* decision. This is important to note given that the early estimates were derived solely on anecdotal observations or poorly developed methodology (i.e. small population samples). Based on this observation it makes sense to take a closer look at Guttmacher Institutes methodology.

The Guttmacher Institute publishes many unsafe, illegal, abortion estimates but often they are devoid of an explicit methodology. One has to trace multiple references to their original sources to see actual methodologies. This gives the appearance that these methodologies are well established and unquestioned. In fact, the Guttmacher Institute often uses the term "facts", such as in a typical publication about "unsafe" abortion "Facts on Induced Abortion Worldwide".[25] Nonetheless, after tracing these references back to their original sources much of the estimates appear to be based directly on incidences of maternal mortality and medical complications and surveys. In the Guttmacher Institute document "Methodologies for Estimating Abortion Incidence and Abortion-Related Morbidity: A Review" there is a considerable discussion about the aforementioned methodologies.[26] There is also a theory by the Population Council that is based on fertility rates. It appears this methodology is used a *validation* of the maternal mortality and survey based theories. It is noteworthy to point out that the Population Council and Planned Parenthood were heavily funded by the Rockefellers for many years. Also, Planned Parenthood created the Guttmacher Institute to provide relevant data to support its goal of legalizing abortion. It can be surmised that a separate organization would be more effective in establishing itself as a *credentialed* source of estimates of illegal abortion of and maternal deaths attributed to abortion and that such an organization would be better able to avoid the natural suspicion of impropriety because of a shared political agenda. Planned Parenthood openly funded the Guttmacher Institute for many years. The reality is the Guttmacher Institute is nothing more than the propaganda arm of Planned Parenthood and has used pseudoscience just as Planned Parenthood's founders had in order to advance their common agenda of abortion on demand.

Ironically, the Guttmacher Institute's estimates are still championed as established and authoritative in spite of the fact that they are the result of an untested theory that has not gone through the normal rigors of peer review. Unfortunately, due to the nature of the research industry practically being void of funds for politically sensitive topics, these baseless estimates have been able to go virtually unchallenged (until fairly recently). Furthermore, this *non-science* is still used by the US, UN, and WHO as justification for the promotion of the legalization of abortion around the world where it is illegal or restricted due to the belief that legalizing abortion decreases the number of total abortions. In addition, the *Roe v. Wade* decision depended in large part on the Guttmacher Institutes and Planned Parenthoods illegal abortion and maternal death estimates. The end result is that the promulgation and acceptance of Planned Parenthoods' and Guttmacher's baseless propaganda has greatly impacted the spread of abortion around the world.

In the next chapter, we will look closely at the traditional illegal abortion estimates and compare them with more recent studies and an altogether new methodology to determine the real extent of induced abortion where it is outlawed or restricted.

CHAPTER SIX

A COMPREHENSIVE APPROACH TO ILLEGAL ABORTION ESTIMATES

I n the previous chapters, we saw how early illegal abortion estimates soon developed into a means to an end at the expense of scientific protocol. More precisely, initially figures were used as leverage to allow for the discussion of birth control (which was still illegal at that time). Later, as the barriers to birth control fell illegal abortion estimates were used effectively to moralize the legalization of abortion on the grounds that women's lives would be saved due to reduced maternal mortality rates. Recognizing that Sanger's initial goal was the legalization of abortion and it is apparent the illegal abortion debate dominance was planned in advance by those groups that saw abortion as an ideological imperative for their plan to check world population growth. The monopolization of abortion discourse has continued to this day with the Guttmacher Institute being the prime source frequently referenced by the US, UN and its subsidiaries such as numerous NGO's in Latin America. The consequences are that abortionists are able to influence public policy decisions to such a degree that legal abortion has become an important goal of all the aforementioned groups.

It has now come to the point that it is now being labeled as a basic *human right.*

But what if current illegal abortion estimates are still not established on scientifically sound footing? What if the same overwhelming desire by early eugenists to control the world's population to the point that professional protocol was thrown out the window somehow has been allowed to remain to this day? The implications would be that the argument to legalize abortion is without foundation and worse has become entrenched in public policy in most, if not all, *First World* countries. This is, in fact, what has happened as we shall see.

Until fairly recently, there have been no major studies that challenged the rates that the Guttmacher Institute publishes (this includes US backed research). However, the Melisa Institute in Chile has been publishing comprehensive analysis of illegal abortions in Latin America since at least 2012. The founder, Dr. Koch, is a research scientist in the area of epidemiology and molecular biology and is cited as an author or contributing author in hundreds of published papers registered in the *US National Library of Medicine of the National Institute of Health,* PubMed.[1, 2]

Below is an excerpt from the translated original introduction of a recent study that questions the validity of the Guttmacher Institute's survey methodology for the estimation of abortion in Latin America:[3]

Recently, the Guttmacher Institute estimated a number of 400,400 illegal abortions for Colombia. Given the potential impact that this study could have on various sectors (public and private) it was determined a close look at the published methodology was needed. A summary of the methodology in question is as follows: the authors estimated total spontaneous and induced abortions from the opinions of 289 individuals who work in an equal number of Colombian health institutions through the opinion survey entitled "Health Facilities Survey". Subsequently, an expansive multiplier (x3, x4, x5, etc.) was applied to the survey figures based on the subjective opinions of 102 selected participants in a "Health Professional Survey". There is no objective data based on real events, rather the figures are based on anecdotal estimates from the opinions of the participants. Regarding the public opinion survey methodology, the sampling technique allowed for serious bias in the selection of information. Based on valid epidemiological methods using standardized parameters derived from the particular cases of Chile and Spain as real world models, it was apparent that the Guttmacher Institute methodology overestimates the complications due to induced abortion in hospital discharges by a factor of 9 and the total number of induced abortions by a factor of 18.

It seems apparent the Guttmacher's Institute survey based methodologies are lacking in a sound scientific basis. This is understandable given that the founders of the Guttmacher Institute demonstrated a consistent willingness to promote their agenda of forced world population control at all costs, including the truth and science. Therefore, it is quite logical that the Guttmacher Institute would continue their tradition of propaganda and thus promote rates of illegal abortion that are generally much higher than rates where abortion is legal.

Regarding the aforementioned study by the Melisa Institute the particular cases of Chile and Spain are quite useful for the prediction of illegal abortion. In the case of Chile, abortion was initially made legal in 1931 under a socialist government, but was eventually completely outlawed in 1989. Chile also has very high standards of medical records, which included the many years when abortion was legal. This is a very useful as a tool to infer induced abortion incidence in relation to the number of live births and hospital admissions. In the case of Spain, abortion became completely legal in 1987 and has increased considerably since that time. According to the Melisa Institute, the number of legal abortions in 1987 in Spain is likely a representative figure of the number of illegal abortions prior to 1986.[4]

The Melisa Institute uses the aforementioned analysis and other considerations to project illegal abortion rates for various Latin American countries. Combining this information with census data and the Population Abortion Rate for each country for each period can be calculated, as shown below:[5]

TABLE 5 - COMPARISON OF PUBLISHED AND MELISA INSTITUTE PAR ESTIMATES

Country	Year	Pop.(M)	Legal	Gutt. Inst.	Melisa Inst. low	high
Spain	1987	38.631	43	-	-	-
Argentina	2000	36.903	-	1,211	-	44
Brazil	1991	152.154	-	949	-	47
Chile	1990	13.214	-	1,211	27	54
Colombia	2008	45.153	-	887	23	47
Dominican Rep.	1990	7.245	-	1,132	-	46
Guatemala	2003	12.063	-	538	-	45
Mexico	2006	112.117	-	647	-	47
Peru	1989	21.326	-	1,271	-	46

Only the low illegal abortion figures were projected for Chile and Colombia but this nonetheless is a useful figure to establish a realistic range of abortions in Latin American countries where it is still illegal. Averaging the low and high figures separately based on their differing methodology and we have a range of twenty-five to forty-seven. On the other hand, the range of values offered by the Guttmacher Institute is from 540 to 1,300.

The Guttmacher's Institute's methodology of relating illegal abortion to maternal mortality is based on the notion that a significant number of maternal deaths are caused by illegal abortion. While this makes sense from a logical point of view, in that it stands to reason that a dangerous surgical procedure such as illegal abortion could be the cause of high incidences of maternal injury or death, especially with primitive equipment, the issue of accuracy is of paramount importance. After all, a low number of maternal deaths could demonstrate the illegal abortion incidence is very low. Obviously, if the goal is to create a moral impetus for the legalization of abortion, it makes more sense to demonstrate high maternal mortality rates that are directly caused by a corresponding high rate of illegal abortion. That is the precise tactic that Sanger and other eugenists employed in the early 1930's. In fact, high maternal mortality rates would eventually be an essential moral justification for making abortion legal in the US in 1973 as well as the promotion of abortion's legalization around the world today.

Nonetheless, in the recent Melisa Institute study "Fundamental discrepancies in abortion estimates and abortion-related mortality: A reevaluation of recent studies in Mexico with special reference to the International Classification of Diseases" we find the Guttmacher Institute's traditional claims regarding maternal mortality and abortion are without merit.[6] Particularly, we see that the Guttmacher Institute's illegal abortion figures derived from maternal mortality are up to ten times more than the actual numbers based on an exhaustive review of medical records.[7] This is possible because the Guttmacher Institute comes up with maternal mortality estimates and then applies very high factors to produce final estimates of illegal abortion. The justification for these exaggerated inflationary factors is that abortion is always underreported, which was always Margaret Sanger's mantra.

Furthermore, we also observe from the Melisa Institute study that legal prohibition of abortion is not related to high maternal mortality figures.Specifically, as noted previously, Chile made abortion illegal in 1987 and yet maternal mortality rates have continued to drop to a point that they are at the lowest levels anywhere seen in the world.[8, 9]

Finally, with respect to the notion that legalizing abortion reduces the number of abortions, we find this claim is without merit given that abortion has steadily increased in Spain and Mexico where it was legalized in 1987 and 2007 respectively.[10, 11] This should come as no surprise given that abortion increased dramatically in the US when it was legalized in 1973. It should be clear by now that the Guttmacher's illegal abortion estimates are highly questionable, to say the least.

We shall now look at the fertility based methodology promoted by the Population Council who, like Planned Parenthood and its derivative the Guttmacher Institute, was heavily funded by the Rockefellers for many years.

The idea of trying to determine the principal causative factors of fertility rates came to prominence at the same time Margaret Sanger and Planned Parenthood were finally openly promoting the legalization of abortion in the early 1950's. An early, often-cited work is "Social Structure and Fertility: An Analytic Framework".[12] Not surprisingly, both authors, Kingsley Davis and Judith Blake were proponents of population control and were a married couple. Davis, for his part, was a eugenist and supported abortion as a birth control method and believed in forced sterilization.[13, 14]

Eventually the Population Council would take up the cause of identifying the principal factors of fertility rates. This should be of no surprise given that Davis and the Population Council ran in close circles and had a shared goal of reducing the world's population. To this end the Population Council would make abortion one of the primary factors of fertility rates when it published the work *Fertility, Biology and Behavior: An Analysis of the Proximate Determinants* in 1983.[15] This is significant because the Guttmacher Institute cites this methodology as verification for its flawed illegal abortion estimates.

The primary concept behind this methodology is that the total fertility rate is dependent on a few primary causative factors, known as proximate determinants, and as such any other factors are not taken into consideration. The total fertility rate, TFR, is the number of children a women would be expected to have in her lifetime. This relationship is expressed as follows:

FIGURE 3 - TOTAL FERTILITY RATE FORMULA

$$TFR = C_m \times C_c \times C_a \times C_i \times TF$$

The term "TF" represents "total fertility", which is the maximum theoretical number of children a women could have.

Also, given that each of the above coefficients generally cannot exceed a value of 1.0 and it becomes clear that the value of TFR is always less that the maximum theoretical number of children a woman could have.

The four coefficients, proximate determinants, are the indexes of marriage, contraception, induced abortion, and postpartum infecundability. The index of marriage has to do with the delay of the married union starting from the assumed earliest age of marriage, which is generally assumed to be fifteen years. The coefficients of contraception and induced abortion are dependent on their specific assumed incidence. Postpartum infecundability is the reduction of fertility due to mostly breastfeeding. There is also an upper age limit for the model, which is generally forty-four or forty-nine years. Thus, the age range for this model is generally fifteen to forty-four or forty-nine years.

Abortion's inclusion as a primary factor of total fertility is predictable given the ideological purpose of the Population Council. However, once becoming familiar with the proximate determinates methodology and historical fertility rates, it becomes apparent that abortion is not significant in populations with high fertility rates. This important fact is even pointed out by the one of the authors of the referenced model in a later work. Here is an excerpt:[16]

In pretransitional societies the prevalence of contraception (and induced abortion) is typically negligible, so that fertility can be considered natural . . .

Negligible in the context of the article unequivocally implies that that abortion is not to be taken into consideration for the purposes of analysis of fertility. This conclusion is very important given that Margaret Sanger and other racist Malthusiasts have long promoted that abortion was a significant feature of society, to the point that is was even *natural*. In fact, the Guttmacher Institute promotes this very same theory today, and it is clearly apparent in all of its illegal abortion estimates. Given the wide disparity between the Population Council's research and the constant claims by the Guttmacher Institute, it appears the fact that abortion is not significant in pre-transitional societies has flown under the radar.

Therefore, while the Guttmacher institute chose the proximate determinants model in order to confirm (and thus legitimize) it's published illegal abortion rates, the reality is that this model has completely undermined said rates. Specifically, acknowledging that the incidence of abortion is not significant in pre-transitional societies due to its incompatibility with high fertility rates and that there are still countries in the world today that meet this designation, it becomes clear the Guttmacher Institute's illegal abortion rates for these countries are without merit. Furthermore, recognizing that all societies were at one point pre-transitional and it is evident that significant abortion has not been a *natural* feature of the human existence because any society that embraced abortion would have assured its eventual demise due to abortion's detrimental effects on its fertility rate. The term *significant abortion* is henceforth the incidence of abortion that would cause a noticeable drop in fertility rates. This information clearly shatters Planned Parenthoods long held claim that abortion is an *innate* action on the part of women.

Regarding the demarcation point for rates of fertility where abortion is considered negligent, from Bongaarts' aforementioned work it can be inferred that this would have been around 6.5 births per women per lifetime.[17] This figure can also be derived from the observed TFR rates of the Hutterites. The Hutterites were a group of devout Christians from the US whose fertility rates were closely investigated from 1926 to 1950. Also, of considerable importance is that there were no perceivable occurrences of abortion observed during the period of the study, something that Bongaarts acknowledged:[18]

> *Hutterite women use virtually no contraception or induced abortion, and the age pattern in their marital fertility rates must be consequently be caused by the four remaining proximate determinant: sterility, postpartum infecundability, natural fecundability, and spontaneous intrauterine mortality.*

According to Bongaarts the observed TFR of the Hutterites was around 9.[19] This high TFR was achievable in large part due to lower than normal postpartum infecundability, C_i, which was in turn was a consequence of limited breastfeeding compared to other societies.[20] By adjusting the aforementioned C_i so that it approximates values more generally seen among communities with high fertility rates the TFR is reduced to around 7. This is marginally higher than the 6.5 TFR that Bongaart's recognized as the minimum fertility rate where abortion is negligible but is still a relevant example to demonstrate a relation between high observed TFR's and the lack of induced abortion.[21]

To continue, understanding that societies with TFR's of 6.5 or higher have negligible illegal abortion it makes sense to review historical records of observed TFR's in order to draw a more accurate picture of the historical incidence of significant induced abortion in the world. According to World Bank data, there are currently two countries that have a TFR of 6.5

or higher: Niger and Somalia.[22] Not surprisingly abortion is severely restricted or outright illegal.[23] Looking further back at World Bank statistics from 1960 before the UN's plan of depopulation was in full effect and we see that Sub-Sahara Africa, North Africa, and the Middle East had TFR's of 6.5 or higher. This is quite significant given that these regions include the continent of Africa and all of the Middle East.[24] Also, we see that Latin America and South Asia were not far behind with rates of 6.0 and 6.1 respectively.[25] We must therefore assume that around the year 1960 the incidence of induced abortion in the majority of the developing world at best was not *significant.* This is noteworthy given the populations in these regions, which include all of South and Central America, Africa, the Middle East, India, and South Asia.

The next logical question would be up to what point in time can we infer that induced abortion was negligible in developed regions? According to one source the total fertility rate in the United States at the turn of the nineteenth century was around 7.5, which includes the white and black populations.[26] From this same source we find the birthrate dropped below 6.5 during the 1830's.[27] Regarding Europe's historical birthrates, Western Europe's records are incomplete before the nineteenth century. Nonetheless, it appears the total fertility rate of France and Germany, the two largest countries in Europe, had already dropped below 5.[28] In Eastern Europe and Russia the total fertility rates were approximately 5.8 and 7.5 respectively at the turn of the twentieth century.[29] In summary, we observe it was very likely abortion was negligible prior to 1800 in Western Europe and the early 1900's in Eastern Europe and Russia, while in United States it was not significant prior to 1840.

Now that we see the points in time where abortion was negligible based on the natural constraints of fertility rates the next question is what were the causes of the decline in fertility rates? Previously we mentioned that commonly accepted notion that pre-transitional societies are *less developed* in addition to being devoid of abortion. Conversely, at the opposite end of the scale are countries that fit the designation of post-transitional and are logically *more developed*. the United Nations has standardized these designations as follows:[30]

More Developed Countries = Post transitional
Developing = Transitional
Least Developed = Early transition or pre-transitional

It is quite apparent there is a direct relationship between the level of development in a country and its fertility rate. This seems logical given that the traditional family structure would evolve at the beginning of the early transitional period as women increasingly choose (or felt obliged) to enter the workforce that had traditionally been dominated by men. Also, as we noted in the previous chapter, abortion was beginning to be noticed by medical professionals in areas of high levels of prostitution as the United Stated transitioned to a more industrialized nation, whereas previously this was not the case. So the question remains what portion of the decline of fertility rates in countries transitioning to a more developed state is due to people delaying marriage, having abortions, or other factors? Much has been written about this topic, and not conspicuously abortionists always claim significant levels of induced abortion in all countries, regardless of culture or religion. We now know that claim is without any foundation due to the natural incompatibility of *significant abortion* in pre-transitional societies. Thus, the remaining question is what is the quantification of illegal abortion in countries that are in the phase of transition to a more developed state? Traditionally, this has been deemed an all but impossible task by abortionists like Margaret Sanger and her derivatives at the Guttmacher Institute. Nonetheless, we will subsequently show that illegal abortion rates are indeed constrained by another natural phenomenon and are, in fact, quantifiable by utilizing simple precepts from an established scientific discipline.

Criminology is the scientific study of crime that developed in the early twentieth century. Detailed statistics have been recorded in United Kingdom since 1898 and in the US since 1930.[31, 32] In the US the typical method of presenting crime rates has been using the demographic standard of occurrence per 100,000 population.

Of all recorded crimes, murder is considered to be one of the worst examples, regardless of culture or religion. Logically, a conviction of murder carries a correspondingly severe penalty. On the contrary, crimes such as simple theft are not considered among the worst crimes. Naturally, a conviction of theft overwhelmingly carries a much less severe penalty than murder. By inference one should expect the incidence of theft to be much higher than the incidence of murder, and the facts bear this out. According to 1932 FBI statistics, the US (during the first years' statistics were available and at the height of Sanger's activities) had a murder rate of 8.5 occurrences compared to a larceny-theft rate of 738 for a population of 100,000 persons.[33] In other words, for every murder there were 87 thefts, which is a considerable difference of course. It is readily apparent there is a relation between the severity of a crime and its incidence level. Specifically, as the seriousness of a crime increases its incidence will decrease proportionally. The common term for this is an *inverse proportional relationship.*

Also, crimes of a serious nature do not vary a great deal over time. For example, the murder rate in the US over the last century averaged around 7, with a high of just over 10 and a low of just under 5.[34] Furthermore, the maximum rate estimated for the US was 25 in the late eighteenth century.[35] Worldwide homicide rates are generally less that 50, whereas a rate of 30 is considered relatively high.[36]

Here is a graphic that represents the FBI reported crime rates in 1932 which includes a range of illegal abortion estimates published by eugenists during the same time period as a basis of comparison for discussion:

FIGURE 4 - FBI CRIME STATISTICS FOR 1932

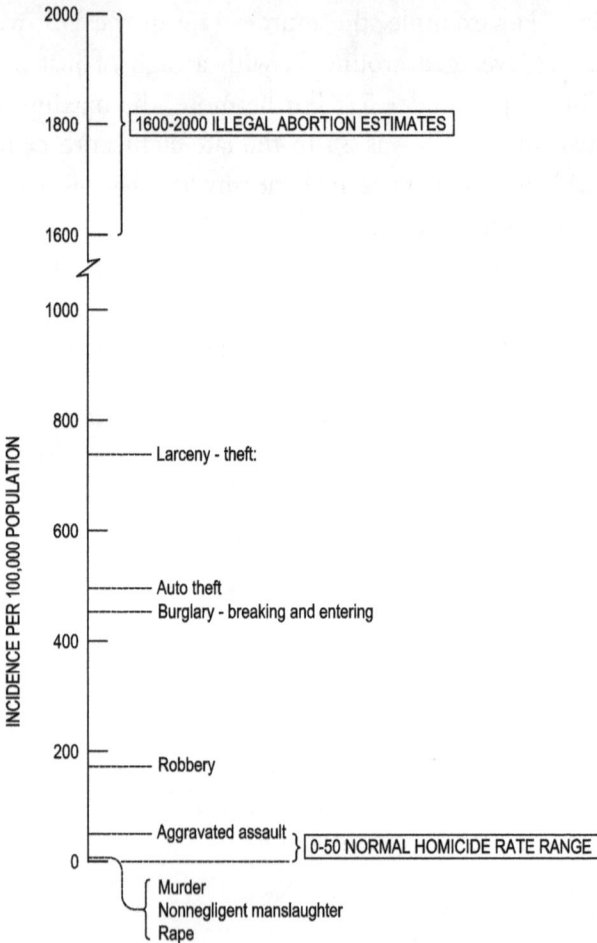

From this graphic, we see that the most severe crimes are located at or near the bottom of the graph while the less severe crimes are located the top. Also, as we progress from the bottom of the graph to the top, the inverse proportional relationship is evident given that the severity of a crime decreases while its incidence increases. Contrasting this we see the Malthusiast's illegal abortion estimates are at incidence levels normally seen for petty crime.

We also note that the normal homicide rate range of 0-50 is located at the extreme bottom portion of the graphic and its associated incidence level is much less than those associated with less severe crimes. Understanding that homicide rates of 20-30 are common in pre-transistional countries with very inefficient law enforcement systems and it becomes clear there is a natural constraint to homicide that prevents it from approaching very high values seen in much lesser crimes. Otherwise if this were not the case, we should expect to see sustained homicide rates of 100+ or more.

Extensive historical worldwide homicide statistics support the notion that there is an inherent constraint to high homicide rates. This natural limit is, in fact, directly tied to society's negative perception of serious crime. On the other hand, if we are to believe the Malthusiast's estimates (Figure 5) we must acknowledge that the US's perception of abortion at this time would have been the equivalent of a petty crime, such as jaywalking. Also, understanding that homicide rates of 1600 to 2000 are not seen in recorded history even for deadly, modern wars such as World War II, estimated to be a minimum of 430 (derived from available estimates[37]) and it is clear the Malthusiast estimates of this period are without foundation.

Regarding evidence of Americans' perception of abortion in the 1930's, Margaret Sanger's herself acknowledged the general public's disdain of abortion in addition to the Catholic Church's fierce moral opposition to birth control, which is considered a much lesser offense than abortion. This should not be surprising given that when abortion did appear in the middle of the nineteenth century, it was severely criticized by social commentators of the era such as Susan B. Anthony as well as the newly formed medical professional associations, such as the American Medical Association.[38] As evidence, here is a publication by the A.M.A. from 1857: *Report on Infant Mortality in Large Cities. The Sources of Its Increase, and Means for Its Diminution.*[39]

> *The moral guilt of Criminal Abortion depends entirely upon the real and essential nature of the act. It is the intentional destruction of a child within its parent; and physicians are now agreed, from actual and various proof, that the child is alive from the moment of conception.*

While the American Medical Association was relatively new, it was indeed quite influential given that it played a role in the proliferation of punitive abortion laws enacted throughout the US in the latter part of the nineteenth century. In fact, by the end of the nineteenth century almost every state had abortion laws and most of these laws saw no legal distinction for the *quickened* status of the child.[40] Also, while it is true that the codification of abortion laws in the US before 1840 were not common, this does not imply that abortion was tolerated to any great degree. Rather, understanding that abortion's incidence in the US was insignificant at the early part of the nineteenth century and there was no need to have codified laws to address this issue. However, once abortion did start to become a social concern, US society reacted accordingly as would be expected as evidenced by the propagation of laws outlawing abortion in the majority of the states. In retrospect, there is no question that by the end of the Nineteenth century abortion was still considered to be a very serious crime the equivalent of homicide.

In summary, it should be clear that in 1932, society's perception of abortion had not changed sufficiently from its equivalence to murder to that of petty crime in the matter of a generation. From this we are obligated to observe that the eugenist's illegal abortion estimates of this time period (1914-1933 – see Table 2) were without any scientific basis.

Furthermore, recognizing that the Guttmacher Institute currently projects abortion rates with values of over 1000 (converted to the PAR standard) for countries where abortion is still considered unequivocally as homicide, it becomes apparent the Guttmacher Institute's estimates are equally without any scientific basis as well. Otherwise we would be compelled to believe that the PAR's in these countries would surpass that of rates seen in World War II by a large margin. Nonetheless, there is very little evidence to demonstrate such bloodshed nor much less societal attitudes that would tolerate such fantastic levels of homicide given that these countries are majority Catholic nations that require Christian education in public schools and have almost two thousand years of unbroken tradition of teaching that life begins at conception.

To continue, we can also use the same aforementioned principles along with observed fertility rates to estimate illegal abortion rates, such as in the US prior to the legalization of abortion.

Let's look specifically at this particular case to estimate the PAR from the point abortion was acknowledged as a social issue up until it was legalized. Remembering that significant abortion is incompatible with fertility rates of 6.5 or over and

FIGURE 6 - ESTIMATED AND PROJECTED LIVE BIRTHS, 1800-1850

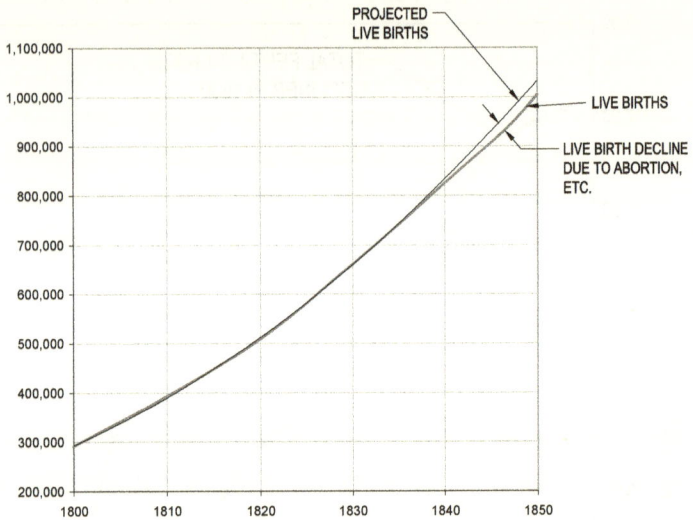

If we choose to assume that the decline in live births is due solely to abortion, then the maximum estimated PAR could be no greater than 55 in 1850. Nonetheless, as we previously noted, US society regarded abortion as a very serious crime, if not the same as homicide. Thus, we could expect its rate of occurrence be equal to somewhat less than 55 but quite possibly higher than the murder rate during this time period, which was about 15.[42] For lack of a more developed methodology we will assume that the PAR in 1850 was an average of these values, or 35. We must also take note that this relatively low PAR would have had a noticeable effect on reducing fertility rates.

Therefore, while it appears certain that abortion did increase after 1830, we also know that abortion, like other serious crimes, would not change to a great degree over time due to the natural limits imposed by society's negative perception. Consequently, we could conservatively expect that the illegal rate could potentially rise from the initial estimated rate of 35 in 1850 to possibly twice that rate, 70, by 1958. This is because up to this point, the legalization of abortion was not openly promoted and thus society's perceptions would not have changed to a great degree. Also, given that a PAR of 70 is the equivalent of very high murder rate only seen in very poor countries with a significant level of civil unrest, we should not expect the illegal abortion rates (PAR) to have exceeded this figure. As additional evidence that a PAR of 70 is more than likely a high figure, we take note that the observed PAR in Spain the first full year after it was legalized was only 43. To continue, while we could expect a nominal increase in the PAR over time up to 1958, after this point the rate more than likely increased at a much higher rate due to active lobbying for the legalization of abortion and the changing attitudes brought on by the sexual revolution of the 1960s. Understandably there are inherent difficulties in projecting what could potentially be an exponential increase in illegal abortion. However, this problem can be skirted by applying a simpler analytical approach. Specifically, by plotting our estimated PAR's up until 1958 and the known PAR in 1970 (when abortion had become partially legal) we can then simply "connect the dots" with a corresponding line. By 1970 the PAR is estimated to be 98, which is derived from recorded data of twenty-one states that had legalized somewhat liberal abortion laws from 1967 and onward.[43] Recognizing that New York and California were among the states that legalized abortion and that both have had historically high incidences of abortion, we can safely assume that the legal PAR would at a minimum represent at least half of the country. Subsequently, by inference we can expect that the illegal PAR would be at the most equal to the legal PAR at this time. Thus, conservatively we can expect the total PAR in 1970 to be 196 (98 + 98).

To review, a PAR of 35 is assumed for year 1850 because it matches the contemporary homicide rate (due to natural societal constraints). From there, one would expect to experience linear increase to a maximum PAR of 70 in 1958 from which as that point there is an anticipated exponential growth (due to the aforementioned manipulations of public perception) until 1970, as represented in the graphic below:

FIGURE 7 - HISTORICAL PAR FOR THE US

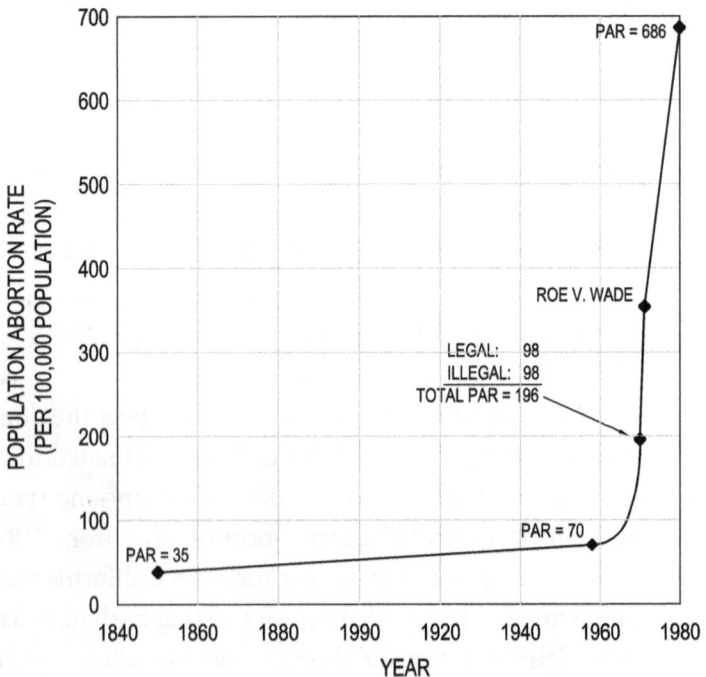

To summarize, we see that illegal abortion rates in the US were subject to and thus limited by the natural phenomenon of high fertility rates and societies innate negative attitude. Therefore, we can expect the PAR to match historical homicide rates (which general range from 5–25 throughout much of history over the last five hundred years) until societies perception of abortion started to change. Furthermore, acknowledging that this change in society's attitude was not a consequence of natural factors but was derived from pressure exerted by population control theorists and the implications become clear – the incidence of abortion in the United States increased artificially due its promotion and eventual legalization.

CHAPTER SEVEN

THE REAL PHENOMENOM OF ABORTION

We saw in the previous chapter that the incidence of illegal abortion is actually subject to constraints, in direct contrast to claims by past and present population control advocates like Margaret Sanger and the Guttmacher Institute. Specifically, high fertility rates preclude significant rates of abortion and society's perception of abortion prevent its incidence from increasing beyond normal levels of homicide (<50 per 100,000 population). However, once the stigma of abortion is removed either by active campaigning or legalization rates it would logically rise.

The dynamic effect of abortion's incidence being directly relatable to society's perceptions is evident in actual recorded cases of abortion's significant increase after its legalization in the cases of the United States, Mexico, and Spain (as previously mentioned). Also, this same dynamic can also be used to predict abortion even where it has been made illegal. For example, after Chile outlawed abortion in 1989, maternal mortality rates experienced a marked decline which implicitly demonstrates a drop in the rate of illegal abortion as well given the innately dangerous nature of illegal abortion procedures.

In this particular case, abortion was legal for many years, thus allowing a more favorable opinion of abortion which would naturally cause an increase in its occurrence. However, when abortion was banned, society's perception once again would have associated abortion with a crime, thus limiting its incidence given its serious nature. It is evident that abortion's incidence is directly tied to society's perception, whether negative or positive in nature, hereby known as the *perception-incidence* relationship.

The correlation between perception and incidence can also be verified by using recorded indicators to predict abortion's occurrence where it is legal. This is effectuated by multiplying society's perception of abortion (for or against, which is readily available from multiple studies) and then multiplying by the number of estimated unwanted pregnancies. In this particular calculation, the underlying concept is that of the number of women that are estimated to have unwanted pregnancies, the percentage that do not see abortion as homicide are the ones that actually procure one, which correlates quite accurately with recorded values, as seen in Table 6 below.[1, 2, 3, 4, 5, 6] For the purposes of comparison a percentage difference from the recorded number of abortions is included as well:

TABLE 6 - LEGAL ABORTION INCIDENCE PREDICTIONS

Country	Year	Live births	%Unplanned pregnancies	%Pro chioce	Predicted Abortions (millions)	Abortions (millions)	% difference
US	1973	3.14	50%	52%	0.815	0.744	10%
US	1990	4.16	50%	65%	1.351	1.610	-16%
US	2006	4.25	49%	49%	1.020	1.212	-16%
Spain	2012	0.45	53%	50%	0.120	0.113	6%

There is a minor amount of error that can be attributed to bias or errors in the input parameters. Nonetheless, considering that the methods offered by Malthusiasts are exaggerated on average by almost 2000 percent more than the legitimate illegal estimates provided by the Melisa Institute (see Table 7 below) and it is evident the *perception-incidence* method offers a superior level of prediction accuracy.[7]

TABLE 7 - ERROR OF PUBLISHED ABORTION ESTIMATES (CONVERTED TO PAR STANDARD)

Country	Year	Pop.(M)	Legal	Gutt. Inst.	Melisa Inst. low	Melisa Inst. high	Min. % difference
Spain	1987	38.631	43	-	-	-	
Argentina	2000	36.903	-	1,211	-	44	2636%
Brazil	1991	152.154	-	949	-	47	1921%
Chile	1990	13.214	-	1,211	27	54	2130%
Colombia	2008	45.153	-	887	23	47	1788%
Dominican Rep.	1990	7.245	-	1,132	-	46	2351%
Guatemala	2003	12.063	-	538	-	45	1094%
Mexico	2006	112.117	-	647	-	47	1268%
Peru	1989	21.326	-	1,271	-	46	2663%

The perception-incidence relationship is quite obviously completely different from the standard accepted *theory* of abortion promoted by population control schemers like Margaret Sanger. This is because the standard theory promotes that abortion has always been practiced by women as a personal means of regulating family size and as such was not subject to cultural perceptions. Nonetheless, there is actually more evidence that demonstrates the perception-incidence relationship's validity as well as the abject failure of Malthusiast estimates.

If it is true that women do kill their children in the womb as a personal measure to limit the size of their families as Sanger and others claimed (and still do), this would implicitly demonstrate a clear perception on the part of the women that abortion was not a serious offence. Therefore, if all barriers to a woman killing her child are taken away, what checks are left in place to prevent women from killing the majority of their children, especially women of low economic status where abortion occurs at the highest levels?

While this may appear to be an inherently difficult question to answer, the reality is that this has indeed already happened on a large scale over a long period of time and has been recorded with a degree of accuracy as well. Specifically, communist Russia legalized abortion after falling sway to Malthusiasts and sexologists. Understanding that the demographic of most of communist Russia started out poor and remained that way until its dissolution and this presents a perfect case study for the observation of abortion and its effects.

Russia had a very high fertility rate of almost 7.5 at the turn of the century which implies no significant illegal abortion incidence. Abortion at this time would have to be assumed to occur at levels associated with homicide due to the perception-incidence dynamic.[8] Artificial contraception was for all intents and purposes nonexistent when abortion was legalized in Russia and remained that way for many years. We also know that even when contraceptives are available, the tendency for women of lower economic levels is to use abortion as a birth control method. Part of the reasoning behind this phenomenon is given that poorer women become pregnant more often (have higher fertility rates[9]) it follows that they would also procure more abortions (where it is legal). Therefore, we should be able to look at Russia's fertility rate over time during this period and associate significant changes with the increased incidence of abortion. While it is true Russia experienced significant industrialization, a natural cause of the decline of fertility rates, it is also a recorded fact that Russia has had one of the highest record abortion rates ever recorded with more than half of all children being killed for many years.[10] Naturally, there should be significant consequences of the majority of Russian women killing the majority of their children. Precisely, the total fertility rate dropped from around 6.4 in 1920 to less than 2 in a matter of fifty years.[11] By all accounts this is the greatest reduction of total fertility rates ever witnessed. It is logical to assume the use of abortion as a birth control method by poor Russian women was a major contributing factor given that abortion was the primary method of limiting family size.

This is undoubtedly compelling evidence that in the absence of the stigmatization of abortion, poorer women would choose to limit the size of their family to a large degree thus causing a significant decrease in fertility rates. Therefore, if we are to believe the standard theory that poorer women are not dissuaded by the legality or perception of abortion and thus kill their children as needed to maintain their desired economic position, we are also compelled to accept that the same poorer women would not be constrained by any other factors that would limit them from having any number of abortions and would indeed choose to have more abortions than children, as is clearly evident in the case study of communist Russia. However, the evidence is clear: all societies at one point in relatively recent history had fertility rates that are not compatible with significant abortion. Thus, we are obliged to recognize that abortion has never been significant at the levels population control theorists would have us believe. On the contrary, if any society did somehow embrace abortion as acceptable we can be assured that over time a significant drop in fertility would occur in line with the Soviet Union, which would eventually cause the society to fail at some point.

Further evidence of the improbability of significant abortion among the poor is the direct relationship between a wealth of a country and its fertility rate: poorer countries have significantly higher fertility rates than richer countries, as clearly evidenced by readily available information from the World Bank. [12] This is only natural understanding that poor countries have none or very few social services. These citizens are obligated to practice the traditional means of planning for the future by having many children to ensure their care in their old age.

It is abundantly clear that the long maintained theory, promoted by Margaret Sanger and the Guttmacher Institute, that abortion is selectively used in all societies at significant levels to limit the size of families fails yet again on the count of being incompatible with historically observed high fertility rates due to abortion's unconstrained nature among poorer women in the absence of stigmatization, such as witnessed in Communist Russia. The reality is that the fact that poorer countries have by far the highest fertility rates in general demonstrates that abortion is greatly stigmatized in these countries and therefore we can be assured that significant abortion does not exist as verified by their observed high fertility rates.

Now that the Malthusian illegal abortion estimates have been completely discredited the question remains: what is the real story of abortion?

As we saw in an earlier chapter, the Catholic Church has long been a consistent and vigorous opponent of abortion that initially manifested itself in doctrine that explicitly recognized abortion as homicide. The Catholic Church later reacted to the increased incidence of abortion by using its influence in majority Catholic countries to have penal codes created to outlaw abortion. Interestingly, the implicit lack of separation of church and state in majority Catholic nations (so championed by secular countries) appears to have been very effective in deterring abortion's legalization. Nevertheless, it is logical that as the Catholic Church waned in influence in the majority of European countries that abortion could be embraced by certain segments of society. The question is when did abortion start becoming enough of a social issue that it merited notice and what were the causes?

While recognizing that illegal abortion rates would have never been significant due to the Catholic Church's influence and confirmed by the inspection of total fertility rates, we might be able to believe that attitudes could change where the Catholic Church was losing its leverage. An example would be during the Reformation in Europe. Nonetheless, one can't expect changes in society's perceptions to happen overnight. After all, the early Protestants were much more Catholic in doctrine and practice than they are today and would have therefore been uniformly opposed to abortion in principle given they had inherited practically the same doctrine and Bible. Indeed, as an example of the Roman Catholic Church's lasting influence even where it had minimal authority, Margaret Sanger herself noted with disdain on more than one occasion the Catholic Church's effective ability to thwart her attempts to promote birth control. This happened, as previously mentioned, at the

Sexual Reform Congress of 1930 in Vienna.[13] This is quite telling given that the Catholic Church has never had great sway in the US, not to mention the fact that birth control is not considered as serious as killing an unborn child. What we can take from this is that the Catholic Church's persuasion would have been felt much stronger where it had an official relationship with a government or a majority population of Catholics. This was precisely the environment Europe had for many centuries, virtually assuring the incidence of abortion was not significant.

Further evidence of this moral opposition is apparent in the history of midwifery in Europe (until it was displaced by the emerging medical professions in the nineteenth century). One example is the 1578 Memmingen ordinance as quoted in "The Art of Midwifery: Early Modern Midwives in Europe":[14]

> *When they become upon a young girl or maid or someone else who is pregnant outside marriage, they should speak to them of their own accord and warn them with threats of punishment not to harm the foetus in any way or take any* bad advice, as such foolish people are very likely to do.

This opposition continues up until the nineteenth century. Nonetheless, as abortion as a social concern arose in the early part of the nineteenth century the cause for its legalization eventually was taken up by eugenists in their drive to depopulate the world and as a direct consequence the historically natural negative perception of abortion was effectively changed over time. The facts surrounding abortion's emergence as a social issue deserve a closer look, especially since we now understand significant abortion has never been a prominent feature of the human experience.

Prostitution has thrived throughout history where displaced men with disposable income have sought out sexual partners. This is especially apparent in port cities throughout the historical world. With the onset of the Industrial Age in Europe and later in the US in the eighteenth and nineteenth centuries, a similar dynamic was created as industrial sectors took root in the bigger cities. Typically, men would leave their homes in the outlying rural areas and move to the cities drawn by the demand for factory labor. Naturally, they would have excess spending money and adequate free time to use it with a certain percentage would seek out prostitutes. Logically, a prostitute would want to procure abortions in order to be able to have sexual relations without becoming pregnant nor much less have the *burden* of a child. The increasing amount of prostitution in major urban areas of the US during the onset of the Industrial Revolution has been discussed at length, such as in the historical account "City of Eros: New York City, Prostitution, and the Commercialization of Sex, 1790-1920".[16]

With the increase of abortions, naturally the first witnesses to this phenomenon would have been doctors working in the relatively new medical disciplines of gynecology and obstetrics. Evidence of this concern is apparent in a document prepared by the recently formed American Medical Association in 1857 titled "Report on Infant Mortality in Large Cities. The Sources of Its Increase, And Means for Its Diminution".[17] Here we see abortion is clearly considered a serious crime which in turn provoked a response by medical professionals. The American Medical Association would become an important activist for the creation of laws in the US to make all abortions illegal.[18]

Susan B. Anthony, a renowned women's suffrage activist, made the observation in 1875 that promiscuity, general immorality, and even part time prostitution and was on the rise in cities due to the replacement of goods and services traditionally attributed to women in her famous "Social Purity" speech:[19]

The prosecutions on our courts for breach of promise, divorce, adultery, bigamy, seduction, rape; the newspaper reports every day of every year of scandals and outrages, of wife murders and paramour shooting, of abortions and infanticides, are perpetual reminders of men's incapacity to cope successfully with this monster evil of society.

The statistics of New York show the number of professional prostitutes in that city to be over twenty thousand. Add to these the thousands and tens of thousands of Boston, Philadelphia, Washington, New Orleans, St. Louis, Chicago, San Francisco, and all our cities, great and small, from ocean to ocean, and what a holocaust of the womanhood of this nation is sacrificed to the insatiate Moloch of lust. And yet more: those myriads of wretched women, publicly known as prostitutes, constitute but a small portion of the numbers who actually tread the paths of vice and crime. For, as the oftbroken ranks of the vast army of common drunkards are steadily filled by the boasted moderate drinkers, so are the ranks of professional prostitution continually replenished by discouraged, seduced deserted unfortunates, who can no longer hide the terrible secret of their lives . . .

. . . In the olden times, when the daughters of the family, as well as the wife, were occupied with useful and profitable work in the household, getting the meals and washing the dishes three times in every day of every year, doing the baking, the brewing, the washing and the ironing, the whitewashing, the butter and cheese and soap making, the mending and the making of clothes for the entire family, the carding, spinning and weaving of the cloth—when everything to eat, to drink and to wear was manufactured in the home, almost no young women "went out to work." But now, when nearly all these handicrafts are turned over to men and to machinery, tens of thousands, nay, millions, of the women of both hemispheres are thrust into the world's outer market of work to earn their own subsistence . . .

Clearly, then, the first step forward solving this problem is to this vast army of poverty-stricken women who now crowd our cities, above the temptation, the necessity, to sell themselves, in marriage or out, for bread and shelter.

It is logical that the byproduct of industrialism in big cities was increased prostitution and promiscuity prompted by *part time* prostitution at levels never seen before in history. Naturally, the result of so many people having sexual relations outside of marriage would create a notable increase of unwanted pregnancies. This clear relationship between promiscuity and abortion during the nineteenth century should come as no surprise given that that current US Center for Disease control abortion statistics demonstrate that unmarried unions are still the overwhelming source of abortions (85 percent).[20]

Still, while the crime of abortion was definitely on the rise in the US in the middle and latter part of the nineteenth century, what was in question was the frequency. From the perspective of a physician in a concentrated urban area like New York City it might appear that abortion had become an epidemic of sorts. However, any urban doctor who would pretend to make inferences of the prevalence of abortion over large disassociated populations based on what amounts to anecdotal data derived from casual observation is problematic to say the least. Yet this is exactly what was done. The problem is that while statistics of other crimes were being recorded during this period, specifically in England,[21] this academic discipline was still in its initial stages of development and its implementation was limited, especially in the US. Therefore, the professionals who were most apt to witness an abortion, medical practitioners, were left with trying to formulate valid estimates of abortion in spite of the fact that they were inadequately prepared to do so. Quite obviously there was a great deal of variation in the estimated extents of abortion.

Nonetheless, while illegal abortion did increase to a certain degree, it could have never approached the rates that the population control advocates constantly promoted. This is because abortion was still considered as a serious crime by the majority of society and as such rates couldn't be expected to exceed homicide rates of relatively violent countries, which are generally less than 50 (as we saw in Figure 6 of the previous chapter). On the other hand, the rates proposed by the Malthusiasts ranged from 2000 to over 3000, which represents an average homicide rate of more than six times that of WWII. So, while there would be an expected increase due to a small criminal element in society that was practicing abortion, this was in reality at an order of magnitude of two times less (50^2) than what was promoted by Sanger and the like, a very significant difference. Of course, when abortion was legalized the perception could change considerably as might be expected; but as we saw earlier, post-legalization rates can still be adequately predicted using the perception-incidence concept. This clearly demonstrates that abortions incidence has always been tied directly to society's perception.

In summary, the overwhelming evidence demonstrates that abortion is constrained by societal attitudes, regardless of the status of legalization. For the particular case of pre-transitional societies, abortion incidence is negligible given its natural incompatibility with high fertility rates, and thus would assume to be at rates comparable to those of criminal homicide. For transitional societies, while it could be expected that the large-scale promotion of abortion might influence the increase of rates, this would in large part still be constrained by the stigma of abortion being illegal and could not be expected to exceed a PAR of 50, due this value being representative of a normal high in observed homicide rates. In the case of post-transitional societies, while PARs can reach very high values compared to normal homicide rates (no conflicts/wars), it can be shown that for the most part these abortions are obtained by the percentage of women that do not see abortion as homicide, thus still demonstrating the effect of the constraints exerted by societal attitudes.

It is evident that Sanger and other Malthusiasts used every means possible to progress their cause to reduce the world's population at all costs, including pseudo science, via the legalization of abortion on demand. Also, it appears evident these same population control advocates purposely influenced the change of the quantification of abortion (from the standard) in order to separate it from other social indicators as well as to associate it with an issue exclusive to women. This paved the way for abortion's evolution from disgrace to *innate right*. But this is not the only reason for abortion's forced separation from other social indicators; it is also now clear that abortion's academic isolation was done purposely to hide abortion's real impact. In fact, the real consequences of abortion have been so great that it completely defies convention. Furthermore, until now this never revealed information would appear to be the primary reason that abortionists are currently spending millions of dollars annually in Latin America to unbelievably promote abortion as a form of *justifiable homicide* while at the same time fighting abortion's designation as a homicide in the United States and Europe.

CHAPTER EIGHT

ABORTION AS JUSTIFIABLE HOMICIDE: REVISED HOMICIDE STATISTICS

O ne can only surmise that when early Malthusiasts were attempting to estimate abortion's incidence in the early 1930s that they must have researched available information, such as that available from the US Bureau of the Census "Vital Statistics". This document was available with comprehensive information regarding deaths since at least 1900 and abortions since 1929. Here they would have seen abortion classified using the standard method of rate of occurrence per 100,000 population. We also might imagine when Malthusiasts were preparing their illegal abortion rates using the same standard classification much to their chagrin they would have observed that their proposed abortion rates were practically double the rate for all of the annual causes of death in the United States at that time. Obviously, this would prove difficult to defend in any unbiased academic environment, anything other than population control conferences that Margaret Sanger was particularly good at organizing. Therefore, abortion estimates would only be presented either as totals or as associated with women or births, but never using the standard format of rate per 100,000 population. We can also expect that these alternate quantifications of abortion statistics was energetically promoted by Malthusiasts and subsequently influenced a fellow population control enthusiast with whom they constantly rubbed shoulders, Halbert Dunn, to change the US government's formal classification of abortion as well.

All these machinations were obviously vital in order to keep abortion's purported incidence completely isolated from other academic disciplines, not to mention politicians and the general public, lest such outlandish numbers might actually be subjected to any real form of critical review. What a grand plan it has turned out to be, given that it took almost seventy years before similar estimates proffered by the Guttmacher Institute would finally be subject to an academic review. It goes without saying that any scholarly challenge could never originate in the US given abortions acceptance by the majority, or at least represented as such by the popular media and subsequently taken as fact.

However, with the Melisa Institute's work and our criminological analysis we can now be confident that significant abortion is a recent phenomenon. This is independently verified by recognizing that historical fertility rates in the majority of countries before the onset of the Industrial Revolution are innately incompatible with significant abortion incidence. Furthermore, while the evidence to support insignificant abortion in pre-transitional societies is without peer, this is only the tip of the iceberg when considering other factors. These include factors that influence primitive total fertility rates that subsequently would never leave room for the rates of induced abortion promoted by organizations that believe it is their right to reduce the world's population at the cost of the truth and human lives. Specifically, according to a study of childbearing in the US going back to 1910, 23 percent of women can be expected to have four or more children. This means it is likely that less than 20 percent of women would generally be expected to have the majority of all children in any given society given that the remaining 80 percent of women could have at most four children on average.[1] Therefore, any significant reduction in the fecundability (fertility performance) of this small segment (such as due to significant abortion) in any given society would disproportionally reduce overall fertility rates which consequently would cause the birth rate to fall, and eventually the particular society in question.

In light of the reality that *casual* abortion is just a figment of the imagination of self-appointed elitists, it only makes sense to call abortion specifically by what it has long been known as; a homicide. This is justified given the fact the theory of casual abortion arose in areas that had a two-thousand-year continuous tradition of recognizing abortion as homicide due to the fact that Catholic countries used church doctrine in place of civil law (due to an implicit lack of church and state). This established a judicial precedence that predates abortion's legalization by almost two millennia – long before abortion's history was systematically rewritten by racist population control theorists.

In order to adequately demonstrate the impact of abortion a distinction between the number of legal and illegal abortion will have to be made. Also, in order to relate abortion and homicide figures together, both legal and illegal estimates will subsequently be converted into "Population Abortion Rates" (PAR) for this purpose using population data. This is necessary in order to finally do that which has purposely long been hidden from public view; compare abortion to other social indicators, specifically homicide, thus demonstrating the real effect abortion has had since its widespread legalization some fifty years ago. With regard to illegal abortion estimates, two sources of information are used. For the countries for which the Melisa Institute has provided high and low illegal abortion estimates a PAR was deduced from the two figures and then used to reconstruct a composite estimate (Argentina, Brazil, Chile, Colombia, Dominican Republic, Guatemala, Mexico, Peru). For the countries that have no reliable formal illegal abortion estimates the PAR was assumed to be that equal to the recorded homicide rate, based on the previously mentioned concept of the "perception-incidence" relationship (Honduras, Venezuela, Ecuador, Nicaragua, Panama, Costa Rica). Not surprisingly, for the majority of the countries whose figures were derived from the Melisa Institute's analysis the illegal abortion estimates are very close to the value of the recorded homicides for their respective countries.For the countries that have higher projected illegal abortion rates than their respective homicide rates this should be assumed to be due to the effect of constant lobbying for the legalization of abortion, such as in Argentina.

The revised homicide statistics in descending order are shown below in Table 8 for year 2003 for selected countries:[2, 3, 4, 5]

TABLE 8 - REVISED HOMICIDE STATISTICS

Country	Pop.(M)	Legal Abortion	Illegal Abortions	Criminal Homicide	PAR	Publish. Hom. Rate	Actual Hom. Rate
Cuba	11.25	151,500		720	1347	6	1354
Russian Fed.	144.67	1,504,000		41,764	1040	29	1068
Estonia	1.37	10,600		151	773	11	784
Hungary	10.13	53,800		223	531	2	533
United States	290.11	1,287,000		16,246	444	6	449
Puerto Rico	3.83	15,600		796	408	21	429
Sweden	8.96	34,400		90	384	1	385
France	62.24	208,800		996	335	2	337
Canada	31.68	104,200		538	329	2	331
United Kingdom	59.65	181,600		1,014	304	2	306
Slovakia	5.37	16,200		145	301	3	304
Norway	4.56	13,800		50	302	1	303
Denmark	5.39	15,600		65	289	1	291
Czech Rep.	10.19	27,100		163	266	2	267
Italy	57.31	132,800		688	232	1	233
Finland	5.21	10,700		104	205	2	207
South Africa	46.13	70,100		19,512	152	42	194
Netherlands	16.23	28,800		211	178	1	179
Belgium	10.38	16,200		228	156	2	158
Germany	82.53	129,300		825	157	1	158
Switzerland	7.34	10,500		73	143	1	144
Honduras	6.63		4,070	4,070	61	61	123
Colombia	41.87		16,197	22,527	39	54	92
Venezuela	25.80		11,351	11,351	44	44	88
Guatemala	12.06		4,214	4,234	35	35	70
Brazil	181.75		54,565	52,527	30	29	59
Dominican Rep.	9.07		2,570	1,905	28	21	49
Mexico	108.06	40,387		10,049	37	9	47
Argentina	37.97		12,738	2,886	34	8	41
Chile	16.00		5,224	512	33	3	36
Peru	27.07		7,545	1,327	28	5	33
Ecuador	13.28		1,939	1,939	15	15	29
Nicaraugua	5.32		633	633	12	12	24
Panama	3.24		337	337	10	10	21
Phillipines	82.60		6,443	6,443	8	8	16
Costa Rica	4.17		300	300	7	7	14
Poland	38.20		649	649	2	2	3
Ireland	4.00		44	44	1	1	2

The first thing that stands out to the observer is that the countries where abortion is legal also have the highest adjusted homicide rates by far. Conversely, some of the traditionally regarded violent countries are in reality among the most peaceful countries in the world. But this is really only the tip of the iceberg.

In 1995, before the World Wide Web really took hold, the Guttmacher Institute estimated there were 26 million legal abortions for a total population of 5.8 billion.[6, 7] While the Guttmacher Institutes illegal abortion estimates have now shown to be unreliable, there is no reason to suspect their legal abortion estimates. If anything, they should be assumed to be lower than the actual values. However, for the purposes of demonstrating abortion's real effect, this difference is of little significance. Interestingly, after 1995 it has been increasingly difficult to find legal abortion totals which will require us to bring together data from others years for our comparison. In 1997 there were a total of 52 million non-abortion related deaths.[8] Just a few years later, in 2000, there were 520,000 homicides and 310,000 war related deaths.[9] Remembering that illegal abortion is constrained by society's perception and we can thus assume that it is no more that the total number of homicides, or around 500,000 per year (maximum, expected to be considerably less after subtracting out conflicts). Therefore, the total deaths for this period are 26 + 52 + 0.5 + 0.3 + 0.5 = 79.3 million. Here it is clear to see the real impact of legal abortion, for our subject period it accounted for a third of all worldwide deaths. Not surprisingly, abortion is the greatest cause of death in the world every year. [10] Also, abortion is also the greatest cause of violent death by a large margin given that the next cause is homicide, at a half a million for the whole world. Furthermore, the calculated homicide rate due to legal abortion worldwide in 1998 was 448, which exceeds that of World War II at 430. This is notable because many countries have virtually no abortion which means many other countries have much higher rates, as demonstrated in Table 8. Also, understanding that modern warfare is much more deadly than historical warfare due to weapons, transportation, and supply efficiency and we can finally see the true impact of abortion. Abortion is the greatest cause of death the world has ever known in terms of rate and magnitude that has no parallel in human history.

We no longer need to wonder how it is possible that fertility rates have fallen well below the supposed replacement rate of 2.1 where abortion is currently legal. Also, there are no longer any questions as to why early illegal abortion estimates were purposely quantified differently than other social indicators like homicide, and why this propaganda tool continues to this day. There is also no doubt now why abortionists are spending millions in Latin America to convince people that the rest of the world sees abortion as the justifiable homicide of children – specifically to have the whole world eventually accept that killing children is a mother's right before anyone ever discovers the real impact. Nonetheless, it was all for naught, soon everyone will know the implications of legal abortion.

CHAPTER NINE

ABORTION HOMICIDE: UNSUSTAINABLE ECONOMICS AND SOCIAL INDICATORS

Now that we have seen that abortion is causing the destruction of human lives at rates never before seen in history, we must suspect that there must be compelling evidence of the corresponding negative effects. A significant reduction in fertility rates has long been attributed to abortion, but what are the other effects on society?

One of the more common discussions of the effects of abortion is the effect on crime. A popular theory maintains that legal abortion actually reduces crime. Not conspicuously the 1972 Rockefeller Commission implied an association with lack of legal abortion and an increase in crime.[1] Another much more specific claim that abortion reduces crime was proposed by John Donohue and Steven Levitt in 2001.[2] From a eugenist's logical standpoint it would appear at first glance that by killing the majority of the children of blacks crime would consequently reduce over time. In fact, the reduction of the children of blacks was the stated goal of white supremacists like Margaret Sanger, who stated the following in an article about racial cleansing - "Birth Control and Racial Betterment":[3]

Like the advocates of Birth Control, the eugenists, for instance, are seeking to assist the race toward the elimination of the unfit.

Eliminating unwanted black children is still the main focus of the current day Planned Parenthood, as is clearly apparent from their slogan "every child a wanted child" and the observation that 79 percent of its abortion facilities are located within walking distance of black neighborhoods.[4, 5] It is no wonder that in these areas more than half of all black children conceived are killed. Therefore, given that blacks are disproportionally involved in crimes it would appear logical to any racist that crime could be reduced by killing a large number of black children or by preventing them from being conceived in the first place. However, this assumption ignores other factors that influence crime as well as the consequences of legalizing the killing of children.

Due to the fact that abortion has been embraced as a human right by the West, we cannot expect to find a great deal of investigation demonstrating the ill effects of abortion to be forthcoming from a research industry that dares not to alienate its primary source of funding (the government and public corporations). Rather, we will have to look at available studies to infer tendencies, relationship, and trends and then subsequently draw our own independent conclusions.

Conspicuously, in the aforementioned study "The Impact of Legalized Abortion on Crime" that purported to show that the legalization of abortion has reduced crime there is no discussion regarding another very important factor related to crime incidence – the cost of law enforcement. It is only logical to include this factor given that it is readily apparent that a better prepared and equipped police force will be more effective at reducing crime. Therefore, any study that would attempt to relate the legalization of abortion and the reduction of crime while offering no analysis of the police budget over the same time period could very well support some false conclusions.

According to the US Census from the period when public order costs were initially recorded in the US, from 1922 to 2010, the greatest increase of police budgets at the Federal, State, and Local levels occurred from 1970 (when abortion was legal in a handful of states) to 1978 when the per capita cost of the combined Federal and State police forces rose more than 144 percent. Furthermore, during this same time period the correction costs (jails and prisons) rose over 300 percent, as shown in the following graphics:

FIGURE 8 - POLICE SPENDING RATE (PER CAPITA)

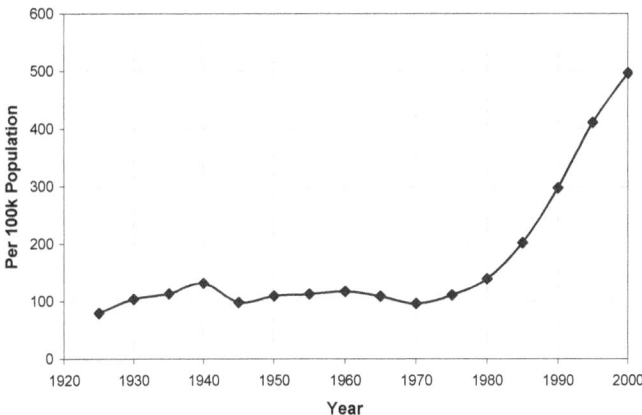

FIGURE 9 - INCARCERATION RATE

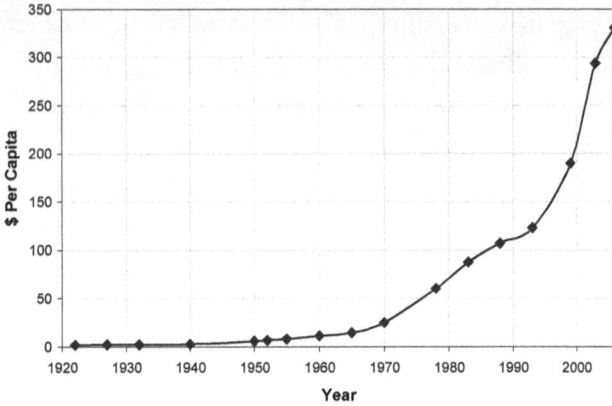

These high rates of increase of law enforcement budgets clearly exceeded inflation at that time (according to the standard historical Consumer Price Index during this period) as well as the normal increase due to population growth, which was fairly constant since 1950. It is only logical to surmise that these historical increases reflect a response to control increasing crime. After all, during this time period police needed significantly more money in order to employ more officers and buy more equipment and more jails and prisons were built to accommodate an ever-increasing number of prisoners. Could the increase of the cost of law enforcement be due to the legalization of abortion and if so, how could abortion be responsible for increasing crime?

Abortion can be seen in one of two ways. For those persons who recognize that a unique human life is created at conception abortion is considered a homicide by the simple definition, whether legal or illegal. For those persons that do not consider that a human life is created at conception there is still the recognition that a *potential human life* begins at conception.

Therefore, abortion is considered the elimination of a person or potential person who is or would be the member of a family, whether it would be just the mother and child. Thus, it should be of no surprise that the family in question would be negatively affected by abortion. A mother that is aware that she has a future child in her womb yet still procures an abortion demonstrates the future child's life has no value to her. A father that takes part in the abortion is also acknowledging the future child in the womb has no value to him. The children of a mother who is visibly pregnant will also be affected by understanding that their sibling has no value to their mother. The end result of abortion is that the value of a child in society is undermined. But not only that, obviously some children would resent their mother/father's decision and this would subsequently erode a child's respect for his/her parents. In summary, abortion devalues children and can affect the innate respect children have for their parents. The overall result would be that the individual family would in many cases degrade from a natural union of refuge that provides moral guidance for children to a mere obligatory structure that ultimately would exert little influence on children's moral formation.

This debilitation of the function of family is indeed a measurable. All we have to do is look at similar historical negative influences on the family to see the short term and long term effects. One particularly relevant example is slavery in the US.

Slavery in the early part of US history was notably vicious compared to other forms of slavery. The historical record establishes that families were frequently broken up by slaveowners. This can be seen in the writings of a noted Abolitionist of the period, Cassius Marcellus Clay:[6]

The master in Russia may make the serf, sow, cut wood, or spin – yet he may not sell him from the soil; the master in Kentucky may do all that the Russian may do; and yet sell the slaves from off the soil, and separate families. Is there an sensible man who fails to see a degree of crime here greater than in Russia?

Here is an excerpt from an article by archeologist Dr. Michael Trinkley of the Chircora Foundation, a historical society located in South Carolina:[7]

How many slaves were sold away from their families? One study, Speculators and Slaves: Masters, Traders, and Slaves in the Old South *by Michael Tadman, suggests that one out of every five marriages was prematurely terminated by sale and that if other interventions are added, the number rises to 1 in 3. In addition, slave trading tore away one in every two slave children under the age of 14.*

Even after slavery was abolished the attack on the black family continued. The Southern Democrat Party formed the Ku Klux Klan and promulgated Jim Crow laws that endured well into the twentieth century. The goal of the latter measures was to repress blacks, which would naturally detrimentally affect the black family. This negative influence is demonstrated by looking at the available social indicators of blacks in the US from the time of the Great Depression to the present day.

For example, according to the FBI's Uniform Crime Reports of 1934, blacks were four to twenty-three times more likely to be involved in the most common crimes than whites. By 2010 the black crime rate had still increased but the factor of incidence compared to whites had decreased for four of the six specified crimes. This decrease in the factor of incidence between blacks and whites should be directly attributed to the fact that almost half of the black children conceived since 1973 had been legally exterminated due to abortion.[8]

TABLE 9 - WHITE AND BLACK CRIME FOR 1940, 1970 AND 2010

| | Crime Rate | | | | | | Factor of Incidence | | |
| | Whites | | | Blacks | | | | | |
Crime	1934	1970	2010	1934	1970	2010	1934	1970	2010
Murder/homicide	3	5	2	27	42	14	10	8	7
Robbery	9	20	19	42	265	159	4	13	8
Assault	6	48	101	126	290	352	23	6	3
Burglary	20	140	74	90	509	230	5	4	3
Larceny	26	327	341	158	1072	933	6	3	3
Prostitution	3	10	13	14	143	67	5	14	5

Promiscuity in the black community has been equally dismal since records were taken in 1940. In 1940 the percentage of births to unmarried black women was 16.8 percent, which at the time was 8.4 times higher than that of whites. In 2010 the black rate had increased to 68.8 percent.[9] There are other as well factors that demonstrate the very poor state of the black family, such as incarceration rates and drug use.

In summary, the purposeful manipulation of the American black family has had a measurable deteriorating effect on the black family, as clearly evidenced by their dismal social indicators. While institutionalized slavery and racism initially eroded the black family, later blacks were targeted by other groups, such as Margaret Sanger, which has allowed the destruction of the black family to continue unchecked to this very day.

Nonetheless, while it is true that abortion was legalized to eliminate blacks and other persons of color, poor whites were targeted as well, after all the goal of Eugenics is the *betterment* of the *races* by *racial cleansing*. Therefore, we should expect a detrimental effect on the white family as well, and subsequently all of society. This dynamic is evident by observing that while the incidence of certain crimes have seen a marginal reduction since the legalization of abortion, the reality is law enforcement budget increases have far outstripped inflation during the same period as well as the normal budgetary increases due to population growth.

However, the damage of abortion isn't limited to individual families and children; the family as it functions in society is also compromised as we shall soon see.

Abortion (as well as birth control) considerably reduces the number of children born every year. This is a direct consequence of the stated goals of the UN's Population Division program of *reproductive health* and by proxy its sexual education program. Their aim is to reduce the Total Fertility Rate of societies to the *minimum* fertility *replacement*. The *replacement rate* is considered to be the minimum number of children the average women should have in her lifetime to *replace* deceased persons. At first glance this seems quite a logical target fertility rate as the theory is that the population would eventually level off to a more or less constant figure. However, this very simplistic approach fails to consider that in order to reach this rate a considerable portion of women and men would not have only one child or none whatsoever. While it is self-evident that low fertility (well below 2.0 such as seen in Europe) would imply a significant number of persons would have only one child, the claim that reducing fertility rates increases childlessness has become a contentious issue among demographers because it would imply a greater burden on social services. Nonetheless, there is a wealth of information to associate low fertility with higher childlessness rates. For example, historical data (US Census and Pew Research Center) show that childlessness was at 10 percent in 1910 for women of forty to forty-four years of age compared to 18 percent in 2008.[10, 11] Therefore, as fertility rates drop we can expect to witness an increase in the number of elderly individuals with one or no children. It should also be expected that this segment of the population would have more difficulty covering the cost of basic needs given they have less supplemental income. Thus, abortion detrimentally affects the function of the family in society as it requires the government to accept an ever-increasing burden of taking care of elderly people that have no children or too few to help them cover the costs of their basic needs. This is a departure from the traditional model where there are relatively few childless elderly individuals who are taken care of by the extended family and is still seen in many areas of the world in countries that have no social service programs for the elderly.

With these observations in mind, it is clear that abortion and birth control polices will eventually require the creation of ample social service programs to take care of the elderly that have none or too few children. Ironically, the UN (through its depopulation programs) implies that the reduction of the fertility rate is the key to economic sustainability. Nonetheless, observing that countries with ample social service programs also have the highest debt to GDP ratios and it can be argued that these countries are hardly sustainable long term. They have instead been able to defer the consequences of their unsustainable policies to some point in the near future. On the other hand, how can much poorer countries be expected to fare as well long-term without the same economic advantages of much more wealthy countries? While it is certain the reduction of the number of children initially would offer poorer countries some economic relief in the short term, the reality is this would be in exchange for the compromise of the traditional family model of taking care of the elderly. This will have long term consequences, none of which are positive. Thus, any less advantaged countries that buys into reducing its fertility rates would in affect be selling their future for the temporary appearance of economic improvement. Furthermore, the destruction of the traditional family model should also be considered a form of wealth distribution given that the government must raise taxes and redistribute them in order to take care of the ever-increasing number of elderly. This is opposed to the traditional model where this burden falls on the extended family. In essence, where depopulation programs are in effect, the family is forcefully redefined and given a lesser role, with long-term consequences such as eventual economic unsustainability.

Not too conspicuously, most demographers and economists would naturally shun claims that depopulation could actually be the cause of obligatory long term economic failure. After all, current depopulation policies, otherwise known as *reproductive health*, supposedly have all *positive* initial tendencies that point to long term economic health. The truth is the effect of such disastrous policies in the West have not yet come to light due to the relatively short period of time of the widespread acceptance of depopulation schemes. However, this is not to say there is no available evidence to dispute *reproductive health* policies. The communist experiment of the USSR is a relevant example of the consequences of the forced subordination of the family and the widespread promotion of reduced fertility rates.

The fall of the USSR has been commonly attributed to many things, except a falling fertility rate. This might seem odd at first as there is significant discussion about the negative effects of the West's falling fertility rates. However, when one factors in the reality that abortion has now been long embraced as a human right and it becomes apparent that any professional that should propose that abortion could be the prime cause of the fall of the USSR would be at best shunned by the scientific community. This is because it would have clear implications for other countries that have similar depopulation programs. The reality is science has ideologically embraced not only abortion but depopulation policies as well. Also, it is not surprising that any demographers that have the ability to influence policy are also depopulation theorists. However, while it was once quite fashionable to openly advocate ethnic cleansing to reduce the world's population, current day demographers have instead quietly shifted away from such an obvious racist stance and instead now promote depopulation as a supposed road map to sustainability. Therefore, lacking in depth analysis of the effect of abortion on the Soviet system we will have to resort to using the available information at hand.

As we explored earlier, abortion clearly undermines the traditional function of the family as a social unit and also as it functions in society. Communism also negatively affects the family; this is partly due to the fact that its ideological purpose is redefined for the benefit of the state. However, the family is still seen as somewhat essential in imparting the state's ideology to children, so we should not attribute any evidence of the degradation of the family solely to communism, but to abortion as well.

While there is relatively little available information regarding arrest rates in the former Soviet Union, there is sufficient information about the Soviet corrections system. Since incarceration rates can be related to the prevention of crime, we can use this information to adequately assess the state of criminal delinquency in the former Soviet Union. Also, there is a common perception that the majority of prisoners in the Soviet Union were due to political imprisonments but the numbers derived from actual recorded data does not bear this out. Specifically, according to the study, "Victims of the Soviet Penal System in the Pre-war Years: A First Approach on the Basis of Archival Evidence", the percentage of political prisoners was generally in the 20 -33 percent range from the period of 1934 to 1953, excepting the period from 1944 to 1948.[12] According to the study "US Rates of Incarceration: A Global Perspective" the incarceration rate of the Soviet Union in 1950 was among the highest ever recorded at 823.[13] Taking into account that 25 percent of the total prisoners were political in nature and the assumed incarceration rate for non-political offenses drops to 618. According to the aforementioned study, this rate is only second to the incarceration rate of 738 for the US in 2006, which was the highest in the world for the most populous countries at that time. When considering the effect that abortion has had on the American black family, it is only logical that the Soviet family would have been equally negatively affected. While one might choose to dispute the portion in which abortion caused the Soviet family to degrade, the reality is it does not take away from the argument that crime will naturally increase when the family is compromised. Furthermore, an increase in crime (or in crime prevention) will require an obligatory increase in spending, which would have exerted a significant strain on the Soviet system. Nonetheless, this is not the only negative economic effect created by legalized abortion.

Most important economic theory depends on the notion of supply and demand. An increase (or decrease) in demand will affect an increase (or decrease) in supply. This theory has been proven throughout the world for millennia, regardless of culture or language. Also, understanding that supply is dependent on labor in order to be able to satisfy demand and it is clear that a decrease in demand will in turn eventually affect a decrease in the labor needed to create the goods or services that are in demand. Significant abortion, such as seen in the USSR, reduced the population of children to a great degree, which in turn reduced the demand of goods and services related to children. This is because in traditional *pretransitional* (before significant abortion) societies infants and children are a majority of the overall population, and as such are significant consumers. The importance of the child population is evident by looking at the distribution of the entire population based on age. The most common graphic used to demonstrate this is called a *Population Pyramid*. The *pyramid* term comes from the fact that the natural distribution of persons in any *pretransitional* population (before significant abortion) is in the form of a pyramid. Attrition (excepting old age) contributes to the shape of the pyramid with the angled sides. Below are the population pyramids for Africa in 1970 and 2014 as seen below from UN data (outline represents 2014):

FIGURE 10 - POPULATION PYRAMID FOR AFRICA

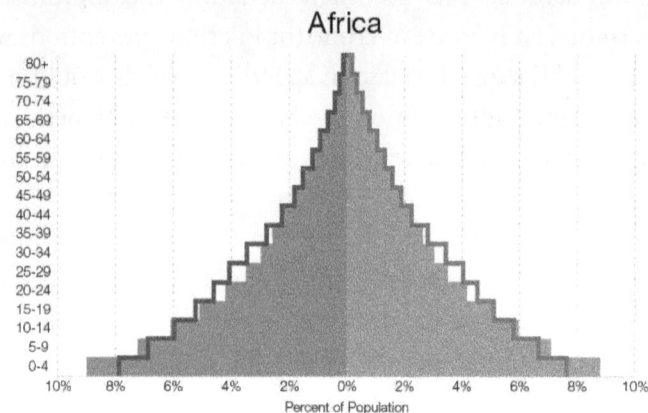

Africa

We see that the sub twenty-year-old population accounts for the majority of persons in Africa between 1970 and 2014. However, where abortion is prominent this is reduced significantly as the lower age ranges are truncated, as shown below in Europe's population pyramid of 1970 and 2010:

FIGURE 11 - POPULATION PYRAMID FOR EUROPE

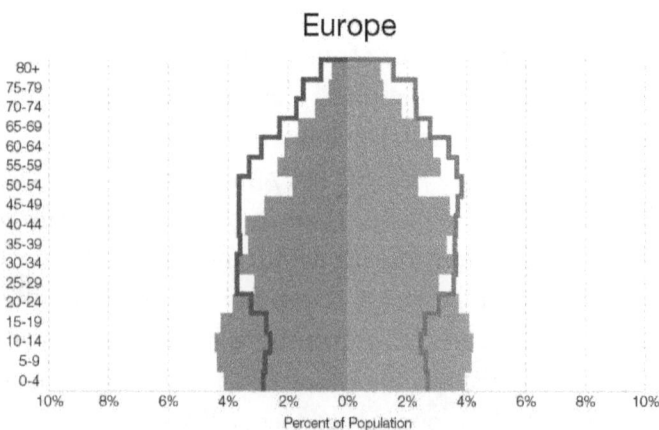

Europe

The absence of the area to the extreme left and right on the lower portion of the graph implies a drastically reduced number of children due to abortion and birth control. In fact, the 0-4, 5-9 and 10-14 groups are all less than the immediately following age groups (when they normally should be greater) thus showing the extreme level at which abortion and birth control have affected the fertility rate.

Ironically, while the UN claims significant abortion has always been a feature of the human experience regardless of culture or religion, the reality is that the UN's own historical population data soundly refutes this claim as witnessed above. This is not to say the UN does not recognize the drop in fertility rates around the world; they do. However, there is no acknowledged connection between the UN's own open depopulation policies via the promotion of abortion and birth control and the results that are clearly visible from looking at past and current population distribution trends.

The reduction of the most significant element in any population would eventually have severe consequences, as was the case in Russia. In fact, the USSR permitted more conceived children to be killed than born for many decades with conservative estimates being that well over two-hundred million lives were lost. Therefore, these lost generations were not able to provide very essential, plentiful, and low cost manual labor services. Thus, the Russian economy would be increasingly straddled with older persons incapable of doing the essential manual labor that any economy needs. As such, Russia's economic output would be severely stunted. Furthermore, these older persons would one day be retirees and this, taken with the fact that the family model had been shattered, meant that not only would large numbers of elderly, childless Russians depend on the government for basic sustenance, but so would those with few children. The evidence of the fall of the economic output was catalogued by the CIA, which created the following graphic that demonstrates the decline of the Soviet GNP that began in the early 1970 (with the USSR GNP as a ratio of the US GNP):

FIGURE 12 - USSR/US GNP

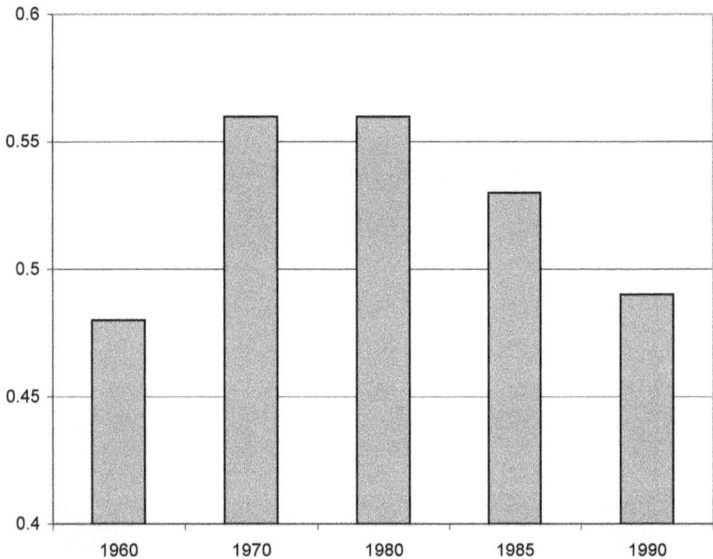

When abortion and birth control are embraced they have immediate effects on society, but these consequences are mitigated because by the appearance of positive economic indicators, specifically the reduction in costs associated with children. This should come as no surprise given that the whole idea of racial cleansing was to lessen the burden on society of *substandard* human specimens. However, as we have seen, the population distribution changes due to the decreased rate of increase in the younger age groups eventually will lead to severe consequences. Also, at some point after abortion and birth control have been embraced the sub twenty population will no longer increase, but start to decrease, as seen in the following graphic:

FIGURE 13 - USSR POPULATION DISTRIBUTION 1950-2010

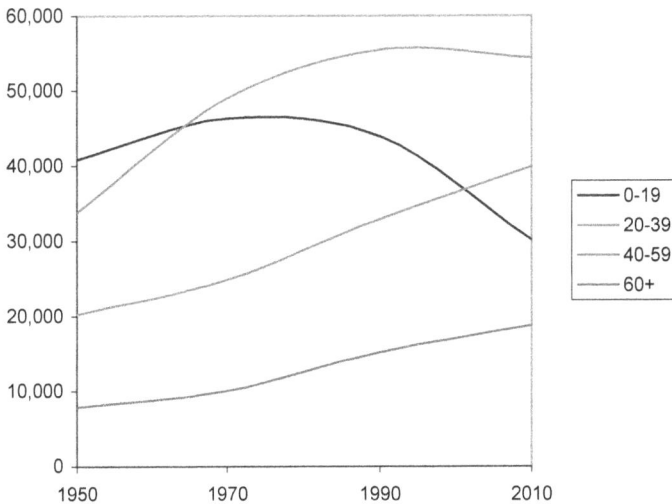

It should not be considered mere chance that the fall of the Russian GNP occurred at precisely the same period that the sub twenty population peaked. This should be directly attributed to the loss of millions of young laborers who were not available to provide the essential services to the Soviet economy, not to mention the economic loss of the goods and service they would have normally consumed. Not surprisingly, eventually Russia would associate the lack of available young men of military age to abortion and would start to make changes to abortion laws to make it increasingly more restrictive as well as offer economic incentives to Russian families to have more children. This was a concerted attempt to undo the damage abortion had wreaked on the Russian system.

Not only has Russia suffered from the USSR's policies, but so have the satellite states that have allowed legal abortion as well. In fact, most of these nations are currently experiencing drops in their population, which is quite predictable. Russia has apparently just recently stopped the reduction of its population by its Herculean effort to all but abolish abortion which has caused abortion rates to fall off dramatically. Nonetheless, the other satellite states that still allow legal abortion with less restrictions than Russia are experiencing a very fast reduction in their populations. This is quite predictable when one understands the domino effect of reducing the sub twenty population which will force a corresponding reduction in the main child producing subsequent age groups. This has obviously had disastrous effects on the local economies not only due to the lack of plentiful young laborers and the goods and services they would normally consume but due to the ever-lessening taxes that can be levied on an ever-reducing populations, all while still having to maintain and repair existing infrastructure. At some point these governments will eventually fail if the fertility rates do not make a marked increase. However, the latter would be virtually impossible lacking individual leaders like Putin that reject modern *reproductive health* (depopulation) policies. It is truly ironic that the term *reproductive health* is used to describe the deadly package of abortion, birth control, and sexual education when the reality is these programs will eventually provoke economic failure at some point after the sub twenty population begins to decline.

In summary, the USSR and American black community provide two solid case studies that clearly demonstrate the long term effects of abortion (as well as birth control). This should not be surprising given that the legalization of abortion forces the redefinition of the traditional family. It also creates obvious economic implications such as increased crime due to the family's reduced ability to impart values as well as the forced redistribution of wealth due to the replacement of traditional role of children caring for parents as well as the increasing number of childless elderly. All of these issues increase the economic burden of any government. While up until now Western governments have been able to mitigate the impending economic effects of abortion because of certain advantages, such as owning the most important monetary systems, their precarious economic outlook is there for anyone to see.

CHAPTER TEN

CAN THE WEAKNESS IN THE FOUNDATION OF CURRENT WESTERN SECULAR MORALITY BE CHALLENGED?

We see how legalized abortion arose from white racists/ elitists who pretended to use the increasing incidence of illegal abortion as a pretext for depopulating the world in order that only the most *fit* of human specimens would remain. While middle and upper class whites were automatically slated for continuing the human race, the same couldn't be said for blacks, or any other persons of color. To this day we find evidence of this fact by the location of the majority of Planned Parenthood's abortion clinics in black neighborhoods. The justification of the targeting of persons based on the color of their skin was based on the *scientific* notion that these persons were little more than socially advanced gorillas. We see how these same racists continued to expand the argument for abortion by broaching it while it was still a very taboo topic under the pretext of abrogating for the promotion of birth control measures. From this fabricated vantage point, high maternal mortality rates would be increasingly introduced to the discussion and attributed to illegal abortion, thus enabling abortion to be gradually identified as a feminist issue. This is contrast to the millennia's long traditional view that abortion was equal to homicide. Later abortion's classification would be changed first in the eugenist community and later by the US government in order that abortion could be completely isolated as a singular issue, thus effectively inhibiting its comparison with other social indicators. These progressive steps were necessary for abortion's evolution to an innate right of women, as it is currently promoted around the world in the present day.

We also see that the white, racist depopulationists were highly motivated in their efforts to rid the world of colored people and with the ample funding of the Rockefeller family, they were able to control the abortion debate. This effective lock on the discourse of abortion would eventually influence the Supreme Court justices so that all pretense of legal precedence and history were conveniently tossed out the window by the rendering of the *Roe v. Wade* decision. We see that once abortion was legalized in the US, abortion would become a women's right and even *cause célèbre*. This, in turn, undermined any interest in the scientific community to challenge the initial justification of the legalization of abortion, high illegal abortion rates, in spite of the fact that these inflated estimates that had not changed in character for almost a century. Furthermore, the scientific community apparently showed little interest in the gross conflict of interest of the primary source of illegal abortion estimates originating from the Guttmacher Institute, even though this organization was created by white supremacists at Planned Parenthood in order to provide propaganda to effectuate the legalization of abortion.

We see that even as history has been rewritten and whitewashed by abortion proponents in order to shore up the *Roe v. Wade* decision, depopulationists have been active in Latin America trying to convince Catholic countries that *advanced* and *modern* countries recognize that a mother has the innate right to take the life of her child. These abortionists have the intention of using any successful promulgated legal abortion laws in coexistence with Human Life law as legal precedence for the future expected challenges to *Roe v. Wade*.

However, once the veil is completely removed from the patchwork and cobbled arguments for abortion, we can see that the *normal* abortion rates proffered by the United Nations are not compatible with observed historical fertility rates, thus ensuring that significant abortion is a recent man made phenomenon wholly enabled by its legalization. Furthermore, with the realization that historical abortion rates mirror historical homicide rates of 1-50 (as opposed to the 500 to 1,500 rates currently promoted by the UN for countries where abortion is illegal) we can be sure that legal abortion is indeed the cause of the greatest sustained loss of life per capita ever witnessed in human history. We can be confident this observation is valid due to the fact that current legal abortion rates are at levels only seen during modern world wars, which due to advantages in terms of weaponry, transportation, infrastructure, and supplies ensures that any prior historical conflicts would have never been able to approach nor sustain death rates seen during modern wars. The result is that the death rates attributed to abortion have no peer in history.

Such is the magnitude of abortion that one is compelled to ask how has it has gone unrecognized as the greatest human tragedy ever to exist when it completely overshadows any other annual cause of death, to include all wars, skirmishes, homicides, terrorist acts, diseases, and famines?

Certainly changing the method of classification of abortion long ago ensured few persons could make equitable comparisons of abortion to other social indicators, but this does not address the ignorance of the magnitude of abortion among persons who would have been exposed to the raw statistics, such as scientists, medical professionals and politicians. While recognizing that the modern scientific community is completely susceptible to political and cultural sensibilities further aggravated by the underlying structure of funding, this does nothing to address the fact that the majority of scientists would have to acknowledge that human life begins at conception and as such also acknowledge that abortion is the equivalent of a legal homicide of an innocent person. It is clear that not only has the abortion argument been manipulated but that ideological agendas have trumped a common sense of morality as well.

It is evident that abortion was clearly enabled by scientists, politicians, and medical professionals who openly rejected the basic human precept of granting the right to exist to each person regardless of color or economic status. The existence of abortion in the present day, despite the availability of compelling evidence of its detrimental effects, demonstrates an ongoing collusion by said professionals that is directly responsible for legal abortion's survival.

Recognizing that the United Nations is the most vocal proponent of *reproductive health* and we must suspect that depopulation has been ideologically and embedded in United Nation policy.

In looking into which parties are directing the United Nations Population Division to continue to coerce countries into reducing their fertility rates, the evidence points clearly to the United States government. It should not be considered mere chance that the US Census Division reclassified abortion at the height of the racist eugenist's activities to legalize abortion but rather purposeful collusion by certain elements in the United States government with depopulationists to advance a global depopulation agenda. After all, during this period the US government was sterilizing women in Puerto Rico under the "Operation Bootstrap" program that eventually affected a third of all Puerto Rican women. While Margaret Sanger did her best to promote depopulation policies, she wasn't the only person to be heavily funded by the Rockefeller's; the Population Council was specifically created in 1952 by the Rockefeller Foundation for the very same purpose of reducing the world's population at all costs. Not surprisingly, the Population Council is still one of the main sources of studies for the United Nations Population Division. Thus, it is apparent that the very same racist depopulationists that started the drive to legalize abortion are still quite active directing the current United Nations depopulation policies. However, since it is no longer fashionable to openly advocate the elimination of colored people racist depopulation policies have been re-packaged as politically correct *reproductive health.*

Nevertheless, the current proponents of *reproductive health* would have us believe that all racist ideologies are a thing of the past. Then again, has Planned Parenthood/ Guttmacher Institute ever acknowledged the depopulationist agenda and disparaging and blatantly racist comments of its founders? Has the Population Council ever acknowledged that their founder was an avid racist depopulationist? Has the

United Nations ever acknowledged the history of abortion as a tool by white supremacists and elitists to depopulate the world?

Further evidence of the assertion that Eugenics is alive and well is the United Nations unwillingness to acknowledge that all overpopulation predictions, the initial justification for abortion and birth control, have consistently failed over the years and continue to do so. In fact, the world still produces much more food than can be consumed. Also, given the overwhelming obesity epidemic in countries that have legalized abortion, it is clear that the amount of food the world produces is many times more than sufficient to adequately provide a healthy amount of daily food for every person, this includes all the lives lost due to abortion. Furthermore, the abject negative consequences of abortion are either ignored or attributed to other factors, such as low fertility rates well below the *replacement* rate, ageing populations in countries where abortion is legal, and falling populations. In addition, abortion's disastrous long term effects on economies and local governments due to the eventual ever lessening demand for goods and services in addition to ever lessening taxes to pay for the ever-increasing ageing population are completely ignored.

Finally, undeniable proof of the embedded depopulationist agenda is the United Nations refusal to acknowledge that countries that embrace *reproductive health* policies have no way to turn back and substantially increase their fertility rates. Thus, birth rates will fall until the economy crashes with no hope of recovery, unless drastic changes are taken, which is the path Russia has chosen to stop its falling population by increasingly limiting legal abortion and paying its citizens to have large families.

Recognizing that the United Nations is all but openly trying to depopulate the world is nothing new. However, up until now few realistic solutions have been proposed or action taken to uproot the very embedded ideological racists in the demographic community that wield almost complete control over the worlds *fertility* policies. Part of this no doubt stems from the perception that the world is indeed overpopulated, in spite of the acknowledged repeated abject failures of overpopulation predictions. Also, the notions that developing countries are mired in political corruption, violence, poverty, and suffering while the West is one of the few refuges left in the world is directly responsible for enabling depopulation policies existence because the latter policies are assumed to be partly responsible for the West's affluence. These perceptions are bolstered by constant studies issued by the United States and the United Nations that paint developing countries as complete disasters in every sense of the word. Thus, there is little doubt why many Westerners would associate *reproductive health* with peace and sustainability, which is the precise perception that the racist depopulationists and their proxy, the United Nations, works so hard to project.

However, the reality is the exact opposite. While the West claims *reproductive health* is the key to sustainability the former communist countries and their falling birth rates tell us a completely different story. While the West has many advantages as mentioned before, how effective can these be to counteract ever increasing social service and law enforcement costs and a lessening tax base in the long run? The reality is long after the West crumbles due to their depopulation policies, developing countries will continue to thrive using the tried and true traditional model that has worked for millennia; have plenty of children to ensure a sound and realistic future. This is opposed to the West's short and unsustainable run of frantic development using the money saved by killing millions of children and preventing millions more from being born.

THE QUESTION NOW IS WHAT CAN BE DONE?

First, acknowledge that there is more than enough evidence to demonstrate that significant abortion (greater than an incidence of 50) rarely or never existed prior to the modern era due to its devastating effects on fertility rates that render them unsustainable.

Second, recognize that legal abortion and birth control will drive countries to economic ruin, as the former communist countries are now experiencing, in spite of all mitigation attempts.

Third, understand that challenging legal abortion in the West will not be possible without effectively challenging secularism. This is because secularists have an ever-increasing iron grip on society, as witnessed by new laws, as well as the commanding ability to influence new generations in US public schools and also by effectively controlling popular media and news agencies and also as a whole support abortion and birth control. In fact, the evidence overwhelmingly demonstrates abortion was only legalized due to the concerted efforts of secularists that continue to this day.

As evidence of the control secularists exert a recent survey shows 62 percent of Americans, aged eighteen to twenty-nine, believe abortion is *not important*.[1] It should not be surprising that young Americans are increasingly pro-abortion given that largest public school union the US, the National

Education Association, voted overwhelmingly for Obama's two presidential bids during their annual meetings.[2, 3]

Once the realities of the consequences of abortion are embraced and the ongoing abortionist lobby is identified, the beginning of the fall of legal abortion can be assured. This is due to a very simple principle that is the foundation of all Western thought and common to secularists and religious alike – the concept of human rights.

Thus, by pointing out to secularists that they are solely responsible for the greatest rate of killing of innocent persons that has ever occurred (based on death rate alone), the door will open to effectively challenging the ever-increasing secular domination in the West, and subsequently legal abortion. Obviously, many will correctly point out that secularists (in the West) do not recognize that a human life is created at conception. Nonetheless, there are many countries that do indeed recognize this as scientific fact such as most of Latin America, parts of Africa, Ireland, and Poland. What would happen if these countries demanded the United Nations include legal abortion rates in the official homicide statistics published every year? This would clearly show that countries with legal abortion suffer from the highest homicide rates in the world, as well as ever seen in human history. Could Western countries effectively challenge this demand in an international court? After all, Western countries have no laws that discuss when human life begins but rather a void that does not address when a human life is created, something pro-life countries most certainly have. In fact, pro-life countries have Human Life laws that are derived from almost two-thousand years of unbroken legal tradition due to their lack of implicit separation of church and state among the Catholic Church and Catholic countries that equate abortion with homicide.

The reality is the West could never hope to challenge any established Human Life law in a legal environment they don't completely control, as evidenced by the concerted and ongoing well organized effort by secularists to defeat any proposed Human Life laws where abortion on demand is currently allowed. This is in addition to secularists trying to convince Catholic countries to pass legal on demand abortion laws in order to establish legal precedence. A successful challenge to published homicide rates would mean the eventual death of legal abortion as the rights of the unborn person would trump any other infringing rights.

Even an unresolved challenge to published homicide rates would be effective simply because of the widespread exposure of the real impact of abortion as well as the realization that secularists alone created this human tragedy. This effect is secured when one understands the dynamics behind secularism's ever increasing appeal in the West.

Secularism has thrived, and will continue to do so, because of the underlying notion that it is as of yet the most superior ideology to exist. This perception is maintained by the popularly promoted idea that the worst offenders of human rights abuses in history are governments that have a close relationship with an organized religion, commonly understood to be past and present Catholic and Muslim states. Thus, while it is recognized that secularism has its disadvantages, it is still perceived to have a net positive effect on the world. This is the precise reason why so many Christians seem resigned to ever lessening religious freedoms (not to mention the redefinition of marriage) because they believe a certain amount of secularism is a necessary compromise for the good of mankind.

However, the reality is that abortion is causing an overwhelming loss of life every year that completely overwhelms any lives saved through military intervention and humanitarian aid by the United States, the European Union, and the United Nations, all secular governments or entities. Specifically, legal abortion accounts for thirty million annual deaths, or a third of all deaths, making it by far the greatest annual cause of death. This is quite significant given that abortion historically matched normal homicide rates, which means illegal abortion should be less than the average 500,000 deaths seen every year due to homicides, wars, and terrorist activities. Ironically, given the astonishing death rate due to abortion we are currently witnessing, it can be stated unequivocally that secularism is the cause of the greatest human rights violation to ever exist, far surpassing any death rates due to Catholic states many centuries ago not to mention deaths due to Islamic terrorism in the present day. In fact, it can be maintained that such is the magnitude of the current rate of the unprecedented slaughter of innocent persons that only the recent modern wars merit any comparison to abortion, while any other causes of death in man's history would have to be omitted due their inherent comparative insignificance.

The implications are clear. Given that secular governments are solely responsible for the magnitude of abortion, we can also rightly claim that secularism as an ideology/philosophy has abjectly failed as well, using the very same standards that secularists pretend to use – the deaths of innocent persons.

By pro-life countries challenging published homicide rates the door would be opened to the undermining of secularism, thereby allowing not only legal abortion to fall but also countries to embrace their religious heritage and pass laws that promote religious values. A domino effect would also be created as secularists would finally have to confront the enormity of the loss of life directly attributed to their ideology, something they have so meticulously mostly avoided up until now at great cost and effort, and subsequently would suffer a severe loss of confidence. *Human Rights* groups like Amnesty International would be completely discredited; after all they support an institution that takes more lives every year than they could hope to save.

Naturally, the initial tendency would be to ignore any international challenge to homicide rates. A media blackout would be expected in the West for most mainstream media. Nonetheless, could the same be said for the countries that would be propelled from among the most violent to the hands down most peaceful countries to exist in the world today? Countries like Honduras or even Venezuela for that matter? Is it possible these countries are tired of being labeled as consistently violent (not to mention persistent human rights violators) that severely hurts not only their voice in the international community but also economically due to the political nature of business negotiations? The fact is these countries are bombarded by studies every year that paint them as corrupt, bloody, and hopeless and it is no wonder why so many of their citizens abandon these countries to go to the *First World*, in spite of having relatively good living standards. The ironic reality is that these countries are more peaceful and sustainable than any country that permits legal abortion. Few know this because of the simple fact that these countries let the children of the poor and minorities live (as opposed to executing them). As a consequence, their nations are fodder for criticism by secularists who point out their *high* homicide rates.

Thus, a challenge to legal homicide rates, while initially expected to be ignored in the Western media, would easily make ground in developing countries. Also, given the inherent nature of the effectiveness of foreign policy being directly reliant on the carefully fabricated perception of superiority and moral authority via constant social indicator studies and it is clear that foreign policy would be degraded significantly, to the point of being relegated to a ceremonial vestige of the past.

Furthermore, given Russia's recent embrace of its Orthodox heritage, to include passing a recent law to protect the Russian Orthodox Church's position as the de facto state religion (something misinterpreted by Western media as an attack on religious freedom instead of a stance against secularism), we can expect legal abortion to one day be abolished in Russia in the near future. What would happen then if Russia joined the developing countries in demanding that official homicide rates include legal abortion? The Western secular machine could no longer ignore this challenge. Further still, what if Russia and other pro-life countries demanded that abortion be recognized as a human rights violation in accordance with international protocol, with the corresponding call for military intervention as a solution to said? After all, the slaughter of innocent children in the West easily supersedes any such event in the history of mankind. As such, it could easily be considered of sufficient urgency to merit immediate action. How could the West respond? What turmoil would be caused in the ranks of normal citizens and leaders that recognize abortion as murder? Who would they support in such a scenario? Abortion would surely be noticed by every politician and citizen.

It is clear that a challenge to official homicide statistics would have far reaching implications, all of which are positive for those who not only oppose the killing of unborn children, but increasing secularism as well. Not only that, but Christians can soundly regain their moral authority by using the very tools that secularists have used to justify their actions, social indicators, by demonstrating that countries that mandate Christian education and protection of the innocent are the most peaceful and sustainable currently in the world.

For those that are not convinced of any countries ability to effectively challenge legal abortion, what other motivation could exist for Americans to once and for all to finally start a movement to demand the fall of abortion? What more than the well documented knowledge that abortion arose among white supremacists and elitists dead set in eliminating persons considered *unfit* for reproduction, and the devastating effect it has had on the black community to the current day? Our fellow black countrymen were once enslaved by white supremacists, and eventually the moral outrage spurred principled Americans to stand up and put their lives on the line for their fellow brethren. Will enough Americans in the present respond to the clear moral disgrace of ethnic cleansing and show that love has no color and take action? History has proven that greatness is not inherited, but is instead a path chosen by individuals that have stood up to gross abuses without withering. Americans have no birthright on which to depend, nor can Americans expect to go unchallenged in this life, as it is innate to our condition, personally or nationally. Rather, freedom constantly depends on individuals that arise to challenges and take the necessary measures to protect the rights of all persons, regardless of color or size.

So, the question is, will abortionists be able to effectively progress the argument for legal abortion to that of a *justifiable homicide*, thus establishing abortion's unchallenged status in the West and predicating the latter's eventual fall, or will courageous individuals once again intervene on behalf of the most innocent persons in society and take action to relegate abortion to the shameful blight as it has always been?

ENDNOTES

INTRODUCTION:

1 John Bouvier, *A law dictionary adapted to the Constitution and laws of the United States of America, and of the several states of the American union; with references to the civil and other systems of foreign law* (Philadelphia: Childs and Peterson, 1856), 775.

2 "The Universal Declaration of Human Rights," United Nations, accessed October 1, 2015, http://www.un.org/en/universal-declaration-human-rights/index.html.

CHAPTER 1:

1 G.M.A. Grube, *Plato, Republic*, (Indianapolis: Hackett Publishing Co. Inc., 1992), 11.

2 "The Code of Hammurabi Project", Yale Law School, accessed October 1, 2015, http://avalon.law.yale.edu/ancient/hamframe.asp.

3 Simon Hornblower, Antony Spawforth, and Esther Eidinow, *The Oxford Classical Dictionary*, 4th ed., (Oxford: Oxford University Press, 2012), 1286.

4   George Mousourakis, *Roman Law and the Origins of the Civil Law Tradition*, (Switzerland, Springer, 2015), 254.

5   Charles Sherman, "Brief History of Imperial Roman Canon Law", *California Law Review* Vol. 7, No. 2 (1919): 94.

6   George Mousourakis, *Roman Law and the Origins of the Civil Law Tradition*, (Switzerland: Springer, 2015), 254.

7   John Locke, *The Second Treatise of Government*, (1690), 4.

8   "The Declaration of Independence: A Transcription", National Archives, accessed October 26, 2015, https://www.archives.gov/founding-docs/declaration-transcript.

9   "Rough draft of the Declaration Of Independence", PBS, accessed October 26, 2015, http://www.pbs.org/wgbh/aia/part2/2h33.html

10 "The Declaration of Independence: A Transcription", National Archives, accessed October 26, 2015, https://www.archives.gov/founding-docs/declaration-transcript.

11 "The Declaration of Independence: A Transcription", National Archives, accessed October 26, 2015, https://www.archives.gov/founding-docs/declaration-transcript.

12 "The Mum Bett Case", Mass. Court System, accessed October 1, 2015, www.mass.gov/courts/court-info/sjc/edu-res-center/abolition/abolition-4-gen.html.

13 "Massachusetts Constitution", The 189th General Court of the Commonwealth of Massachusetts, accessed October 1, 2015, https://malegislature. gov/Laws/Constitution.

14 "Ninth Congress. Sess. II. Ch. 22. 1807", Legis Works, accessed October 1, 2015, www.legisworks. org/sal/2/stats/STATUTE-2-Pg426.pdf.

15 Jonathan Murray, "State v. Mann", North Carolina History Project, accessed October 1, 2015, www. northcarolinahistory.org/encyclopedia/268/ entry/.

16 Jonathan Murray, "State v. Mann", North Carolina History Project, accessed October 1, 2015, www. northcarolinahistory.org/encyclopedia/268/ entry/.

17 Paul Finkleman, "Scott v. Sandford: The Court's Most Dreadful Case and How it Changed History", *Chicago-Kent Law Review* Vol. 82, No. 1 (2006): 4.

18 "History - Brown v. Board of Education Re-enactment", United States Courts", United States Courts, accessed March 4, 2016, http://www. uscourts.gov/educational-resources/educational-activities/history-brown-v-board-education-re-enactment.

CHAPTER 2:

1 Latin Vulgate (Clementine)", accessed January 23, 2016, http://www.drbo.org/lvb/chapter/02021. htm.

2 Brian Clowes, *Abortion, The Facts of Life – 2015 DVD Edition*, (Human Life Institute, 2015).

3 *Corpus Iuris Canonici*, (Academische Druck – U. Verlagsanstalt, 1959), 1122.

4 "Excommunication", New Advent Catholic Encyclopedia, accessed January 23, 2016, http://www.newadvent.org/cathen/05678a.htm.

5 Heinrich Kramer, James Sprenger, *Malleus Maleficarum*, (New York: Dover Publications, Inc. 1970), 80.

6 "L'edict de Roi Henri II", {Bnf Gallicia, accessed January 23, 2016, http://gallica.bnf.fr/ark:/12148/btv1b8620796d

7 Kramer, James Sprenger, *Malleus Maleficarum*, (New York: Dover Publications, Inc. 1970), 80.

8 "L'edict de Roi Henri II", {Bnf Gallicia, accessed January 23, 2016, http://gallica.bnf.fr/ark:/12148/btv1b8620796d

9 "Constitución Apostólica "Effraenatam" contra el aborto", accessed January 1, 2016, Catholic. net, http://es.Catholic.net/op/articulos/5351/enviado5351.html.

10 Donald DeMarco, "The Roman Catholic Church and Abortion: An Historical Perspective - Part I" , Catholic Culture.org, accessed 01/28/2016, http://www.Catholicculture.org/culture/library/view.cfm?id=3361.

11 Jean-Pierre Kintz, "Avortement et Justice", *Annales de Demographie Historique, Societe de Demographie Historique* Vol. 1973 (1973): 401.

12 "CODE PÉNAL DE 1810", Le Droit Criminel, accessed March 8, 2016, https://web.archive.org/web/20160220075012/http://ledroitcriminel.free.fr/la_legislation_criminelle/anciens_textes/code_penal_1810/code_penal_1810_3.htm.

13 "Código penal español: decretado por las Córtes en 8 de junio, sancionado por el rey y mandado promulgar en 9 de julio de 1822", (Madrid, Prensa Nacional, 1822), 76.

14 Judie Brown, "EWTN Catholic Q&A", accessed January 28, 2016, http://www.ewtn.com/v/experts/showmessage_print.asp?number=383314&language=en.

15 Vladimir Lenin, "The Working Class and NeoMalthusianism", Marxists Internet Archive, accessed 10/26/2016, https://www.marxists.org/archive/lenin/works/1913/jun/29.htm.

16 "Roe v. Wade", Cornell University Law School, accessed October 1, 2015, www.law.cornell.edu/supremecourt/text/410/113#writing-USSC_CR_0410_0113_ZO.

17 "American Convention on Human Rights", Deptartment of International Law, OAS, accessed October 1, 2015. www.oas.org/dil/treaties_B-32_American_Convention_on_Human_Rights.htm.

18 "Roe v. Wade", Cornell University Law School, accessed March 7, 2016, www.law.cornell.edu/supremecourt/text/410/113#writing-USSC_CR_0410_0113_ZO.

19 "Legal Scholars" United Sates Conference of Catholic Bishops, accessed October 1, 2015,

http://www.usccb.org/issues-and-action/human-life-and-dignity/abortion/upload/Reactions-of-Legal-Scholars.pdf.

20 Mark Tushnet. "Following the Rules Laid Down: A Critique of Interpretivism and Neutral Principles", *Harvard Law Review* Vol. 96, No. 4 (2011): 820.

21 "Human Life Amendment", Human Life Action, accessed March 7, 2016, http://www.humanlifeactioncenter.org/issues/human-life-amendment.

22 "Written Comments on Protection of the Right to Life from the Moment of Conception in the General Principles Guiding Hungary's Constitution and the proposal of the constitution issued by Fidesz-KDNP March 2011", Center for Reproductive Rights, accessed October 2, 2015, http://www.reproductiverights.org/sites/crr.civicactions.net/files/documents/CRR_HWL_Constitution_comments_Hungary_March_2011FINAL.PDF.

23 "Joint Statement for Human Rights Committee Day of Discussion on the Right to Life", Center for Reproductive Rights, accessed October 2, 2015, www.reproductiverights.org/document/joint-statement-for-human-rights-committee-day-of-discussion-on-the-right-to-life.

24 Victor Alvarez, *Viabilidad jurídica de una Guía Técnica para la interrupción terapéutica del embarazo,* despenalizacion.org.ar, accessed October 2, 2015, http://www.despenalizacion.org.ar/pdf/publicaciones/viabilidad_juridica_peru.pdf

CHAPTER 3:

1 Dona Schneider and David Lilienfeld, *Public Health: The Development of a Discipline, Volume 1*, (Berkley: University of California Press, 2008), 621.

2 "Biographical Sketch", The Margaret Sanger Papers Project, accessed October 13, 2015, https://www.nyu.edu/projects/sanger/aboutms/.

3 "Eugenics", Merriam-Webster, accessed October 13, 2015, http://www.merriam-webster.com/dictionary/eugenics.

4 Francis Galton, *Inquiries Into Human Faculty and Its Development*, (Macmillan, 1883), 17.

5 M. Sanger, "Is Race Suicide Possible", The Margaret Sanger Papers Project, accessed October 13, 2015, https://www.nyu.edu/projects/sanger/webedition/app/documents/show.php?sangerDoc=305433.xml.

6 Margaret Sanger, *Pivot of Civilization*, (New York: Bretanos, 1922), 25.

7 Lothrop Stoddard, *The Rising Tide of Color Against White World-Supremacy*, (New York: Charles Scribner's Sons, 1921), 83.

8 Karen Radar, *Making Mice: Standardizing Animals for American Biomedical Research, 1900-1955*, (Princeton: Princeton University Press, 2004), 93.

9 "Birth Control or Race Control? Sanger and the Negro Project", The Margaret Sangers Papers Project, accessed October 13, www.nyu.edu/projects/sanger/articles/bc_or_race_control.php.

10 Margaret Sanger, *Woman and the New Race*, (New York: Brentano's, 1920), 62.

11 Kathryn Cullen-Dupont, *Encyclopedia of Women's History in America* (London: Routledge, 2002), 202.

12 "Biographical Sketch", The Margaret Sanger Papers Project, accessed October 20, 2015, https://www.nyu.edu/projects/sanger/aboutms/.

13 Margaret Sanger, "Birth Control or Abortion", The Margaret Sanger Papers Project, accessed October 20, 2015, https://www.nyu.edu/projects/sanger/webedition/app/documents/show.php?sangerDoc=232534.xml.

14 Margaret Sanger, "The Pope's Position on Birth Control", The Margaret Sanger Papers Project, accessed October 25, 2015, https://www.nyu.edu/projects/sanger/webedition/app/documents/show.php?sangerDoc=303569.xml.

15 "The Quest for Contraceptive Knowledge: Marking the 80th Anniversary of the Zurich Conference", The Margaret Sanger Papers Project, accessed October 13, 2015, https://www.nyu.edu/projects/sanger/articles/zurich.php.

16 Erna Rieman, "The Vienna Congress", *Birth Control Review* Vol. 14, No. 11 (1930): 321.

17 Germain Grisez, *Abortion: The Myths, the Realities, and the Arguments,* (New York: Corpus Books, 1970) 213.

18 H. Steiner, *Sexualnot und Sexualreform: Verhandlungen der Weltliga für Sexualreform. 4th*

Kongress abgehalten zu Wien vom 16. bis 23, (Wien: Elbemühl Verlag, 1930) 529.

19 Frederick Joseph Taussig, *Abortion, Spontaneous and Induced,* (C. V. Mosby Company, 1936), 448.

20 "International Planned Parenthood Federation", The Margaret Sangers Papers Project, accessed October 12, 2015, www.web.archive.org/web/20130926023208/http://www.nyu.edu/projects/sanger/secure/aboutms/organization_ippf.html.

21 Margaret Sanger, "Birth Control", The Margaret Sangers Papers Project, accessed October 13, 2015, www.nyu.edu/projects/sanger/webedition/app/documents/show.php?sangerDoc=320986.xml.

22 Kathryn Cullen-Dupont, *Encyclopedia of Women's History in America* (London: Routledge, 2002), 202.

23 Edwin Black, "Eugenics and the Nazis -- the California connection", SFGATE, accessed October 13, 2015, http://www.sfgate.com/opinion/article/Eugenics-and-the-Nazis-the-California-2549771.php.

24 Brian Fischer, *Abortion: The Ultimate Exploitation of Women,* (New York: Morgan James Publishing, 2014), 52.

25 Alan Guttmacher. "Family planning; the needs and the methods", *The America Journal of Nursing Vol. 69, No.6* (1969): 1229-34.

26 Donald Critchlow, *Intended Consequences: Birth Control, Abortion, and the Federal Government*

in Modern America, (Oxford: Oxford University Press, 2001), 142.

27 Margaret Sanger, "Love or Babies: Must Negro Mothers Choose", The Margaret Sangers Papers Project, accessed October 18, 2015 https://www.nyu.edu/projects/sanger/webedition/app/documents/show.php?sangerDoc=320905.xml

28 Philip Bump, "Black presidential vote", The Washington Post, accessed October 18, 2015, https://www.washingtonpost.com/news/the-fix/wp/2015/07/07/when-did-black-americans-start-voting-so-heavily-democratic/.

29 "Family Planning - A Special and Urgent Concern", Planned Parenthood, Gulf Coast, Inc., October 18, 2015

30 https://www.plannedparenthood.org/planned-parenthood-gulf-coast/mlk-acceptance-speech.

31 "Birth Control Isn't Genocide", Chicago Tribune, accessed June, 1971, http://archives.chicagotribune.com/1971/06/28/page/20/article/birth-control-isnt-genocide.

32 "1976 Democratic Party Platform", The American Presidency Project, accessed October 18, 2015, www.presidency.ucsb.edu/ws/?pid=29606.

33 Planned Parenthood Targets Minority Neighborhoods – Map Guide", Protecting Black Life, accessed October 14, 2015, http://www.protectingblacklife.org/pp_targets/.

34 S. Cohen. "Abortion and Women of Color: The Bigger Picture", Guttmacher Institute, accessed

October 14, 2015, www.guttmacher.org/pubs/
gpr/11/3/gpr110302.html.

CHAPTER 4:

1 Raymond Bauer, *Social indicators*, (Cambridge:
M.I.T. Press., 1967).

2 *Towards a System of Social and Demographic
Statistics*, (Cambridge, NY: United Nations ,
1975), 3.

3 "Social Indicators", United Nations Statistics
Division, accessed October 15, 2015, unstats.
un.org/unsd/demographic/products/socind/.

4 "Global Health Observatory (GHO) data", World
Health Organization, accessed October 10, 2015,
www.who.int/gho/en/.

5 "Indicators", The World Bank, accessed October
10, 2015, data.worldbank.org/indicator.

6 Robert Nisbet "Social science", Encyclopedia
Britannica, accessed November 03, 2015, http://
www.britannica.com/topic/social-science.

7 Robert Kuczynski, "The Registration Laws in
the Colonies of Massachusetts Bay and New
Plymouth,". *Publications of the American Statistical
Association* Vol. 7, No. 51 (1900): 1.

8 "Census of Population and Housing", United
States Census Bureau, accessed October 10, 2015,
http://www.census.gov/prod/www/decennial.
html.

9 *Historical Statistics of the United States: Colonial
Times to 1970*, (Washington: Bureau of the
Census, 1975), 408.

10 *Mortality Statistics 1929*, (Washington: Bureau of the Census, 1929).

11 "Uniform Crime Reports", The Federal Bureau of Investigation, accessed October 10, 2015, https://www.fbi.gov/about-us/cjis/ucr/ucr.

12 "A Summary of Recorded Crime Data from 1898 to 2001/02", Official Statistics, accessed November 10, 2015 (website) https://www.gov.uk/government/uploads/system/uploads/attachment_data/file/116649/rec-crime-1898-2002.xls.

13 "Criminal and Judicial Statistics: 1800 to present day: Home", Oxford Libguides, accessed November 10, 2015, http://ox.libguides.com/crimstats.

14 *2012 Global R&D Funding Forecast*, (Batelle, 2011), 6.

15 *2012 Global R&D Funding Forecast*, (Batelle, 2011), 12.

16 *Corporate Quality Index,* (HRC, 2015).

17 "Profile - Buyers Guide", Human Rights Campaign, accessed October 11, 2015, http://www.hrc.org/apps/buyersguide/profile.php?orgid=14285.

18 "Changing Attitudes on Gay Marriage", Pew Research Center, accessed October 11, 2015, www.pewforum.org/2015/07/29/graphics-slideshow-changing-attitudes-on-gay-marriage/.

CHAPTER 5:

1 Medical record; a journal of medicine and surgery Vol. 43, (1893): 691.

2   Margaret Sanger, *The Case for Birth Control*, (New York, The Modern Art Printing co., 1917), 195.

3   Hans-Walter Schmuhl, The Kaiser Wilhelm Institute for Anthropology, Human Heredity and Eugenics, 1927-1945, (Netherlands: Springer, 2008) 19.

4   "The Birth of Sexology", The Kinsey Institute, November 03, 2015, https://web.archive.org/web/20160404232034/http://www.kinseyinstitute.org/resources/sexology.html.

5   Margaret Sanger, "Birth Control or Abortion", The Margaret Sangers Papers Project, accessed January 24, 2016, https://www.nyu.edu/projects/sanger/webedition/app/documents/show.php?sangerDoc=232534.xml.

6   "Newsletter #11 (Winter 1995)", Margaret Sanger Papers Project, accessed January 24, 2016, https://www.nyu.edu/projects/sanger/articles/recently_discovered_letters.php.

7   William Robinson, The Law Against Abortion: Its Perniciousness Demonstrated and Its Repeal Demanded, (New York: The Eugenics Publishing Company, 1933).

8   Abraham Jacob Rongy, *Abortion: Legal or Illegal?*, (New York: Vanguard Press, 1933), 103.

9   Margaret Sanger, "National Security and Birth Control", The Public Writings and Speeches of Margaret Sanger", accessed January 24, 2016, https://www.nyu.edu/projects/sanger/webedition/app/documents/show.php?sangerDoc=236613.xml.

10 Frederick Joseph Taussig, Abortion. *Spontaneous and Induced: Medical and Social Aspects*, (St. Louis: C. V. Mosby, 1936) 24-26.

11 "Roe v. Wade", Cornell University Law School, accessed January 24, 2016, www.law.cornell.edu/supremecourt/text/410/113#writing-USSC_CR_0410_0113_ZO.

12 Medical record; a journal of medicine and surgery Vol. 43 (1893): 691.

13 Frederick Joseph Taussig, *Abortion. Spontaneous and Induced: Medical and Social Aspects*, (St. Louis: C. V. Mosby, 1936) 24-26.

14 Margaret Sanger , "Birth Control, A Changing World Attitude", The Public Writings and Speeches of Margaret Sanger, accessed February 5, 2016, https://www.nyu.edu/projects/sanger/webedition/app/documents/show.php?sangerDoc=141309.xml.

15 "Mortality Statistics 1929", *Bureau of the Census* (Washington: Gov't Printing Office,1932) 100.

16 "Vital Statistics of the United States 1946 ", *Federal Security Agency*, (Washington: Gov't Printing Office, 1948).

17 "Birth Control Organizations", The Margaret Sanger Papers Project, accessed February 5, 2016, https://www.nyu.edu/projects/sanger/aboutms/organization_cmh.php.

18 Halbert Dunn, "Frequency of Abortion: Its Effect on Maternal Mortality Rates" (paper presented at the conference "The Abortion Problem", National Committee on Maternal Health, Inc., at the New

York Academy of Medicine, June 19th and 20th, 1942)

19 "Roe v. Wade", Cornell University Law School, accessed February 5, 2016, www.law.cornell.edu/supremecourt/text/410/113#writing-USSC_CR_0410_0113_ZO.

20 Thomas Paul Werner, Ph.D., The well role ideal type theory: A companion to Parsons sick role ideal type in the social system, (Fielding Graduate University, 2009), 22.

21 "Reproductive Justice: Expanding Our Social Calling", Unitarian Universalist Association, accessed February 6, 2016, http://www.uua.org/sites/live-new.uua.org/files/documents/washingtonoffice/reproductivejustice/curriculum/4-1.pdf.

22 "Unitarian Universalist official stands on issues related to women's health and reproductive rights", Houston Unitarian Universalists, accessed February 6, 2016, http://uuhouston.org/uuv4j-uua-women

23 "Abortion Ratios Worldwide in 2008", The Guttmacher Institute, accessed February 6, 2016, https://www.guttmacher.org/media/resources/abortion-ratios.pdf.

24 "Unsafe abortion - Global and regional estimates of the incidence of unsafe abortion and associated mortality in 2008", World Health organization, accessed February 14, 2016, http://apps.who.int/iris/bitstream/10665/44529/1/9789241501118_eng.pdf.

25 "Facts on Induced Abortion Worldwide", The Guttmacher Isntitute, accessed February 14, 2016, http://www.guttmacher.org/pubs/fb_IAW.html.

26 Susheela Singh et al, Methodologies for Estimating Abortion Incidence and Abortion-Related Morbidity: A Review, (Guttmacher Institute, 2010), 49-61.

CHAPTER 6:

1 "Elard Koch", Linkedin, accessed February 14, 2016 https://cl.linkedin.com/in/elard-koch-92102137.

2 "Search results for Koch E", PubMed, accessed February 14, 2016, http://www.ncbi.nlm.nih.gov/pubmed/?term=Koch%20E[auth].

3 Elard Koch et al, "Sobrestimación del aborto inducido en Colombia y otros países Latinoamericanos", *Ginecología y Obstetricia de Méxic* Vol. 80, No. 5 (2012): 360.

4 Elard Koch et al, "Sobrestimación del aborto inducido en Colombia y otros países Latinoamericanos", *Ginecología y Obstetricia de Méxic* Vol. 80, No. 5 (2012): 368.

5 Elard Koch et al, "Sobrestimación del aborto inducido en Colombia y otros países Latinoamericanos", *Ginecología y Obstetricia de Méxic* Vol. 80, No. 5 (2012): 371.

6 Elard Koch et al, "Fundamental discrepancies in abortion estimates and abortion-related mortality: A reevaluation of recent studies in Mexico with special reference to the International Classification

of Diseases", *International Journal of Women's Health*, (2012): 613-623.

7 Elard Koch et al, "Fundamental discrepancies in abortion estimates and abortion-related mortality: A reevaluation of recent studies in Mexico with special reference to the International Classification of Diseases", *International Journal of Women's Health* (2012): 613.

8 Elard Koch et al, "Sobrestimación del aborto inducido en Colombia y otros países Latinoamericanos", *Ginecología y Obstetricia de México* Vol. 80, No. 5 (2012): 366.

9 "Maternal mortality ratio (modeled estimate, per 100,000 live births)", The World Bank", accessed February 18, 2016, http://data.worldbank.org/indicator/SH.STA.MMRT.

10 Elard Koch et al, "Fundamental discrepancies in abortion estimates and abortion-related mortality: A reevaluation of recent studies in Mexico with special reference to the International Classification of Diseases", *International Journal of Women's Health* (2012): 615.

11 Elard Koch et al, "Sobrestimación del aborto inducido en Colombia y otros países Latinoamericanos", *Ginecología y Obstetricia de México* Vol. 80, No. 5 (2012): 369.

12 Kingsley Davis, Judith Blake, "Social Structure and Fertility: An Analytic Framework", *Economic Development and Cultural Change* Vol. 4, No. 3 (1956), 211-235.

13 David Heer, *Kingsley Davis: A Biography and Selections from His Writings*, (New Brunswick: Transaction Publishers, 2004), 444.

14 John Aird, Slaughter of the Innocents: Coercive Birth Control in China, (AEI Press, 1990), 118.

15 John Bongaarts, Robert Potter, Fertility, Biology and Behavior: An Analysis of the Proximate Determinants, (New York: Academic Press, 1983).

16 John Bongaarts, "The Proximate Determinants of Exceptionally High Fertility", *Population and Development Review* Vol. 13, No. 1 (1987): 133.

17 John Bongaarts, "The Proximate Determinants of Exceptionally High Fertility", *Population and Development Review* Vol. 13, No. 1 (1987): 135.

18 John Bongaarts, Robert Potter, Fertility, Biology and Behavior: An Analysis of the Proximate Determinants, (New York: Academic Press, 1983), 12.

19 John Bongaarts, Robert Potter, Fertility, Biology and Behavior: An Analysis of the Proximate Determinants, (New York: Academic Press, 1983), 8.

20 John Bongaarts, Robert Potter, Fertility, Biology and Behavior: An Analysis of the Proximate Determinants, (New York: Academic Press, 1983), 8.

21 John Bongaarts, "The Proximate Determinants of Exceptionally High Fertility", *Population and Development Review* Vol. 13, No. 1 (1987): 133.

22 "Fertility rate, total (births per woman)", The World Bank, accessed February 25,2016, http://data.worldbank.org/indicator/SP.DYN.TFRT.IN.

23 "The World's Abortion Laws 2016", Centers for Reproductive Rights, accessed February 25, 2016, http://worldabortionlaws.com/map/.

24 "Fertility Rate", Catholic Medical Quartely, accessed February 25, 2016, www.cmq.org.uk/CMQ/2013/Feb/crisis_of_declining_human_fertil.html

25 "Fertility Rate", Catholic Medical Quartely, accessed February 25, 2016, www.cmq.org.uk/CMQ/2013/Feb/crisis_of_declining_human_fertil.html

26 Michael Haines, "The Population of the United States, 1790-1920", *Massachusetts: National Bureau of Economic Research*, (1994), Table 3.

27 Michael Haines, "The Population of the United States, 1790-1920", (*Massachusetts: National Bureau of Economic Research*, 1994), Table 3.

28 "France is growing while Germany is shrinking", Max Planck Institute for Demographic Research, accessed 02/27/2016, http://www.demogr.mpg.de/en/news_press/news_1917/france_is_growing_while_germany_is_shrinking_3098.htm.

29 "Fertility Decline and Recent Changes in Russia: On the Threshold of the Second Demographic Transition", Rand Corporation, accessed February 27, 2016, http://www.rand.org/pubs/conf_proceedings/CF124/CF124.chap2.html.

30 "How can you use demographic statistics in public health programs and studies?", PopFam, accessed February 27, 2016, http://www.columbia.edu/itc/hs/pubhealth/modules/demography/useStats.html.

31 "A Summary of Recorded Crime Data from 1898 to 2001/02", Official Statistics, accessed November 10, 2015 (website) https://www.gov.uk/government/uploads/system/uploads/attachment_data/file/116649/rec-crime-1898-2002.xls.

32 "Uniform Crime Reports", The Federal Bureau of Investigation, accessed March 8, 2016, https://www.fbi.gov/about-us/cjis/ucr/ucr.

33 "Uniform Crime Reports", The Federal Bureau of Investigation, accessed March 8, 2016, https://www.fbi.gov/about-us/cjis/ucr/ucr.

34 Claude Fischer, "A crime puzzle: Violent crime declines in America", The Berkley Blog, accessed March 8, 2016, http://blogs.berkeley.edu/2010/06/16/a-crime-puzzle-violent-crime-declines-in-america/.

35 Claude Fischer, "A crime puzzle: Violent crime declines in America", The Berkley Blog, accessed March 8, 2016, http://blogs.berkeley.edu/2010/06/16/a-crime-puzzle-violent-crime-declines-in-america/.

36 "Intentional homicides (per 100,000 people)", The World Bank, accessed March 9, 2016, http://data.worldbank.org/indicator/VC.IHR.PSRC.

P5?order=wbapi_data_value_2012+wbapi_data_value&sort=desc.

37 "By the Numbers: World Wide Deaths", The National WWII Museum, accessed March 9, 2016, http://www.nationalww2museum.org/learn/education/for-students/ww2-history/ww2-by-the-numbers/world-wide-deaths.html.

38 "Social Purity", PBS, accessed November 13, 2015, http://www.pbs.org/stantonanthony/resources/index.html?body=social_purity.html.

39 "A.M.A. Against Abortion American Medical Association opposed Abortion", Horatio Robinson Storer, M.D. (1830-1922), accessed November 13, 2015, http://horatiostorer.net/AMA_vs_Abortion.html.

40 "Roe v. Wade", Cornell University Law School, accessed March 9, 2016, www.law.cornell.edu/supremecourt/text/410/113.

41 Michael. Haines, "The Population of the United States, 1790-1920", (*Massachusetts: National Bureau of Economic Research*, 1994), Table 3.

42 Claude Fischer, "A crime puzzle: Violent crime declines in America", The Berkley Blog", accessed March 8, 2016, http://blogs.berkeley.edu/2010/06/16/a-crime-puzzle-violent-crime-declines-in-america/.

43 Judith Bourne et al., "Surveillance of Legal Abortions in the United States, 1970", *Journal of Obstetric, Gynelogic and Neonatal Nursing* Vol. 1 (1972): 26.

CHAPTER 7:

1 Lawrence Finer, Mia Zolna, "Unintended pregnancy in the United States: Incidence and disparities, 2006", *Contraception* Vol. 84, No. 5 (2011): 478–485.

2 "Table 1-1. Live Births, Birth Rates, and Fertility Rates, by Race: United States, 1909-2000", Centers for Disease Control and Prevention, accessed March 26, 2016, http://www.cdc.gov/nchs/data/statab/t001x01.pdf.

3 Silvia Ponteverda, "Los nacimientos en España suben un 0,1% en 2014 tras cinco años de caídas", El Pais, accessed March 26, 2016, http://politica.elpais.com/politica/2015/06/22/actualidad/1434967590_232915.html.

4 "Cada año se producen en España 240.000 embarazos no deseados", ABC, accessed March 26, 2016, http://www.abc.es/sociedad/20130928/abci-embarazos-nodesados-espana-201309271815.html.

5 "U.S. Attitudes Toward Roe v. Wade ", The Wall Street Journal, accessed 03/26/2016, http://online.wsj.com/public/resources/documents/info-harris0503.html.

6 Carmen Moran, "El 60% de la población apoya la ley de aborto vigente", El Pais, accessed March 26, 2016, http://politica.elpais.com/politica/2014/06/27/actualidad/1403891547_421330.html.

7 Elard Koch et al, E. Koch et al, "Sobrestimación del aborto inducido en Colombia y otros países

Latinoamericanos", *Ginecología y Obstetricia de Méxic* Vol. 80, No. 5 (2012): 371.

8 "Fertility Decline and Recent Changes in Russia: On the Threshold of the Second Demographic Transition", Rand Corporation, accessed March 23, 2016, http://www.rand.org/pubs/conf_proceedings/CF124/CF124.chap2.html.

9 "Fertility rate, total (births per woman)", The World Bank, accessed October 25, 2016, http://data.worldbank.org/indicator/SP.DYN.TFRT.IN?.

10 Anatoly Karlin, "The Rapid And Mostly Unnoticed Decline Of Abortion In Russia", Antony Karlin, accessed October 25, 2016, http://akarlin.com/2013/02/the-rapid-and-mostly-unnoticed-decline-of-abortion-in-russia/.

11 "Fertility Decline and Recent Changes in Russia: On the Threshold of the Second Demographic Transition", Rand Corporation, accessed March 23, 2016, http://www.rand.org/pubs/conf_proceedings/CF124/CF124.chap2.html.

12 "Fertility rate, total (births per woman)", The World Bank, accessed October 25, 2016, http://data.worldbank.org/indicator/SP.DYN.TFRT.IN?.

13 Herbert Steiner, *Sexualnot und Sexualreform: Verhandlungen der Weltliga für Sexualreform. 4th Kongress abgehalten zu Wien vom 16. bis 23,* (Wien: Elbemühl Verlag, 1930): 529.

14 Hilary Marland, *The Art of Midwifery: Early Modern Midwives in Europe*, (London: Wellcome Institute for the History of Medicine, 1994), 86.

15 H. Marland, *The Art of Midwifery: Early Modern Midwives in Europe*, (London: Wellcome Institute for the History of Medicine, 1994), p. 93.

16 Timothy Gilfoyle, *City of Eros: New York City, Prostitution, and the Commercialization of Sex, 1790-1920*, (W. W. Norton & Company, 1994).

17 "A.M.A. Against Abortion American Medical Association opposed Abortion", Horatio Robinson Storer, M.D. (1830-1922), (website) http://horatiostorer.net/AMA_vs_Abortion.html (accessed 11/13/2015).

18 "Writing and links related to Dr. Storer and the Physicians' Crusade Against Abortion", Horatio Robinson Storer, M.D. (1830-1922), accessed November 13, 2015, http://horatiostorer.net/Home_Page.html.

19 "Social Purity", PBS, accessed November 13, 2015, http://www.pbs.org/stantonanthony/resources/index.html?body=social_purity.html.

20 "Abortion Surveillance — United States, 2011", Morbidity and Mortality Weekly Report, Centers for Disease Control and Prevention, accessed Novemeber 13, 2015, http://www.cdc.gov/mmwr/preview/mmwrhtml/ss6311a1.htm.

21 "Criminal and Judicial Statistics: 1800 to present day", Oxford Libguides, accessed November 02, 2015, http://ox.libguides.com/crimstats.

CHAPTER 8:

1 Sharon Kirmeyer, Brady Hamilton, "Childbearing Differences Among Three Generations of U.S. Women", *U.S. Department Of Health And Human Services* No. 68 (2011), 2.

2 Elard Koch et al, "Sobrestimación del aborto inducido en Colombia y otros países Latinoamericanos", *Ginecología y Obstetricia de Méxic* Vol. 80, No. 5 (2012): 371.

3 "Population, total", The World Bank, accessed June 6, 2015, http://data.worldbank.org/indicator/SP.POP.TOTL.

4 Gilda Sedgh et al, "Legal Abortion Worldwide: Incidence and Recent Trends", *International Family Planning Perspectives* Vol. 30, No. 3 (2007), 106–116.

5 "Intentional homicides (per 100,000 people)", The World Bank, accessed June 25, 2015, http://data.worldbank.org/indicator/VC.IHR.PSRC.P5.

6 Ina Warriner, Iqbal Shah, *Preventing Unsafe Abortion and its Consequences*, (The Guttmacher Institute, 1995), 37.

7 "50 Facts: Global health situation and trends 1955-2025", World Health Organization, accessed April 3, 2016, http://www.who.int/whr/1998/media_centre/50facts/en/.

8 "50 Facts: Global health situation and trends 1955-2025", World Health Organization, accessed April 3, 2016, http://www.who.int/whr/1998/media_centre/50facts/en/.

9 Etienne Krug, et al., "World report on violence and health", World Health Organization, accessed April 3, 2016, Geneva, http://apps.who.int/iris/bitstream/10665/42495/1/9241545615_eng.pdf, 7.

10 "50 Facts: Global health situation and trends 1955-2025", World Health Organization, accessed April 3, 2016, http://www.who.int/whr/1998/media_centre/50facts/en/.

CHAPTER 9:

1 "Population and the American Future", The Rockefeller Commission Report, accessed June 13, 2016, http://www.population-security.org/rockefeller/001_population_growth_and_the_american_future.htm#TOC.

2 John Donahue, Steven Levitt, *The Impact of Legalized Abortion on Crime*, The Quaterly Journal of Economics, Vol. CXVI, No. 2 (2001): 1.

3 Margaret Sanger, "Birth Control and Racial Betterment", The Public Writings and Speeches of Margaret Sanger, accessed June 25, 2016, https://www.nyu.edu/projects/sanger/webedition/app/documents/show.php?sangerDoc=143449.xml.

4 "Wanting Every Child to be a Wanted Child", Life News, accessed 06/25/2016, http://www.lifenews.com/2011/10/14/every-child-a-wanted-child-a-pro-abortion-deception/.

5 Planned Parenthood Targets Minority Neighborhoods – Map Guide", Protecting

Black Life, accessed June 24, 2015, http://www. protectingblacklife.org/pp_targets.

6   Horace Greeley, The Writings of Cassius Marcellus Clay Including Speeches and Addresses (New York: Harper and Brothers, 1848), 428.

7   Michael Trinkley, "South Carolina – African-Americans – Buying and Selling Human Beings", SCIWAY, accessed 07/04/2016, http://www. sciway.net/afam/slavery/flesh.html.

8   "Uniform Crime Reports", Federal Bureau of Investigation, 1940, 1970 and 2010.

9   "Nonmarital Childbearing in the United States, 1940–99", National Vital Statistics Reports Vol. 48, No. 16 (2000), 29-31

10 Historical Statistics of the United States: Colonial Times to 1970. (Washington: Bureau of the Census, 1975), 54.

11 Gretchen Livingston, D'vera Cohn "Childlessness Up Among All Women; Down Among Women with Advanced Degrees" Pew Research Center, accessed July 7, 2016, http://www.pewsocialtrends. org/2010/06/25/childlessness-up-among-all-women-down-among-women-with-advanced-degrees/.

12 J. Arch Getty, Gábor T. Rittersporn, Viktor N. Zemskov, "Victims of the Soviet Penal System in the Pre-War Years: A First Approach on the Basis of Archival Evidence", American Historical Association Vol. 98, No. 4 (1993): 1039.

13 Christopher Hartney, "US Rates of Incarceration: A Global Perspective", The National Council on

Crime and Delinquency, November (2006), 3.

14 Chapter 10:

15 Michael Lipka. "5 facts about abortion", Pew Research Center, accessed October 1, 2015, www. pewresearch.org/fact-tank/2015/06/11/5-facts-about-abortion/.

16 Will Potter, "Educators Vote to Endorse Obama"., National Education Association, accessed October 2, 2016, www.web.archive. org/web/20150319165852/http://www.nea.org/home/11058.htm.

17 Ramona. Parks-Kirby, "NEA delegates vote to support President Barack Obama in re-election bid" , National Education Association, accessed October 2, 2016, www.web.archive. org/web/20150319194435/http://www.nea.org/home/46078.htm.

WORLD AHEAD *press*

Self-publishing means that you have the freedom to blaze your own trail as an author. But that doesn't mean you should go it alone. By choosing to publish with WORLD AHEAD PRESS, you partner with WND—one of the most powerful and influential brands on the Internet.

If you liked this book and want to publish your own, WORLD AHEAD PRESS, co-publishing division of WND Books, is right for you. WORLD AHEAD PRESS will turn your manuscript into a high-quality book and then promote it through its broad reach into conservative and Christian markets worldwide.

IMAGINE YOUR BOOK ALONGSIDE THESE AUTHORS!

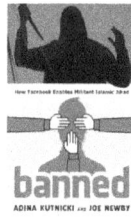

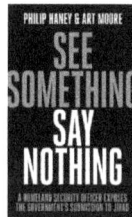

www.ingramcontent.com/pod-product-compliance
Lightning Source LLC
Chambersburg PA
CBHW022359280326
41935CB00007B/239